Part Bible study, part writing tutorial, and part therapy session. In *Restory Your Life*, Mary DeMuth takes each of us by the hand and introduces us to the person God created us to be. With honest hope, she nudges us toward the telling of us, the ultimate offering of our rediscovered being in our world.

> **ELISA MORGAN**, author of *When We Pray like Jesus* and president emerita of The MomCo

Mary can speak to wounds in a way that few can but everyone needs. She is relatable and sincere and will bring truth in the spaces that feel most broken. She is gifted, and God is using her in beautiful ways.

> **JENNIE ALLEN**, *New York Times* bestselling author and founder of IF:Gathering

Whatever hard story you were given, it need no longer define or limit you. Open these pages and walk with Mary DeMuth as she guides you in discovering the better story God is writing through your life. You'll emerge from this deep soul work renewed, with fresh biblical wisdom, clearer purpose, and redemptive joy. Take the journey! You'll never look back.

> **LESLIE LEYLAND FIELDS**, author of *Nearing a Far God* and *Your Story Matters*

Restory Your Life will help you discover meaning in the worst moments in your past and find beautiful next steps for following Jesus with your whole heart. Mary DeMuth guides the reader with kindness, generosity, wisdom, and understanding. I felt seen, known, and loved as I read this book. Your story is still being told, and God has big plans for your future. Highly recommended.

> **MATT MIKALATOS**, author of *God with Us* and *Praying with Saint Nicholas*

Neurobiologically, we are shaped by story. But just as the brain can change, so can our understanding of our stories. In *Restory Your Life*, DeMuth reminds us, "We may be broken by our stories, but God knows how to reframe them." Through both narrative and structure, DeMuth shares a message that is practical, hopeful, and desperately needed.

JESSIE CRUICKSHANK, neuroecclesiologist, speaker, and author of *Ordinary Discipleship*

How Jesus Reframes Your Past, Rewrites Your Present, and Redefines Your Future

Restory your life

MARY E. DEMUTH

Restory Your Life: How Jesus Reframes Your Past, Rewrites Your Present, and Redefines Your Future

marydemuth.com

A NavPress resource published in alliance with Tyndale House Publishers

The Team:
David Zimmerman, Publisher; Caitlyn Carlson, Acquisitions Editor; Elizabeth Schroll, Copyeditor; Lacie Phillips, Production Assistant; Ron C. Kaufmann, Cover Designer; Brandi Davis, Interior Designer; Sarah Ocenasek, Proofreading Coordinator

Direct quotations in the Scripture retellings at the beginning of each chapter are taken from the *Holy Bible*, New Living Translation.

In quoted Scripture with italics or bold, emphasis was added by the author.

The author is represented by Joy Eggerichs Reed of Punchline Agency.

URLs referenced in this book were verified as live and accurate source material prior to publication. Some links may have expired or redirected since publication.

Some of the anecdotal illustrations in this book are true to life and are included with the permission of the persons involved. All other illustrations are composites of real situations, and any resemblance to people living or dead is purely coincidental.

For information about special discounts for bulk purchases, please contact Tyndale House Publishers at csresponse@tyndale.com, or call 1-855-277-9400.

ISBN 979-8-89802-008-8

Printed in the United States of America

32 31 30 29 28 27 26
7 6 5 4 3 2 1

To my new family at Redeemer Rockwall,

who stitched me up and put me back together again.

Contents

[illegible]

[illegible] self-editing your [illegible]

[illegible] monster, [illegible]

In short, you may try to [illegible]

[illegible]

[illegible] what kind of difficulties and obstacles you faced. Did you have a mom[illegible] of profound change? And what does your life look like now that you've learned so much and you're helping others with their restorying?

The chiastic structure may take a little more thought. What wa[illegible]

[illegible]

INTRODUCTION

Origin Story

Time makes up the pages that will be your story. Every time your life changes, you start a new chapter. To me, there's nothing more depressing than someone getting to the end of their days and realizing they've only written one long, boring passage.

ELIZABETH ISAACS, *THE LIGHT OF ASTERIA*

Re-. Inhale. *Story.* Exhale. *Restory.* Breathe.

The word came to me like a respiratory sort of prophecy. Jesus had written an utterly new story in my life, but I was sensing a deeper calling into the healing journey. He invited me into a rewritten story. A repurposed story. A renewed story. A *restory*.

We all have stories: some tragic, some sane, some wild, some tame. But the underlying beauty of all our stories is Jesus' intersection with them—and what he fashions out of the torn pieces.

He cut through mine when I was fifteen years old. The previous three years had brought me to the brink of suicide and a spiral of loneliness, anxiety, and undiagnosed depression. An only child haunted by far too many secrets, I spent those early adolescent years nearly completely alone, isolated on ten acres under the wink of Mount Rainier. My mom tackled master's-level courses late into the evening; my stepdad worked a swing shift at the county jail—all while my unworthiness and shame shouted in the silence. Voices that sounded like mine, but louder, declared my worthlessness. I felt haunted by long-term sexual abuse, indifferent neglect, multiple divorces, drug abuse in the home, and the death of my predatory biological father. Addicted to the quite-available porn in my home, tempted by the marijuana therein, and battling a ragged longing for a father—all these realities ate away at me. My soul felt dry-rotted. My story boasted one long narrative of tragedy, full of far too much trauma to process at fifteen years old.

I didn't know why I'd been born.

The only logical explanation I could deduce was this: I existed to either be stolen from or outright ignored.

One autumn weekend, I found myself nervously stepping into the evergreen air of Camp Timberlake. The Young Life camp situated itself neatly into the too-tall woods not far from my home—yet a lifetime away. Here, leaders listened to me. Peers befriended me. Echoes of Jesus made my heart pound, and I kept crying for no apparent reason. I couldn't get enough of this Jesus. While many reveled in capture the flag or crazy competitions involving shaving cream and mud, I could not wait for the part where we heard about Jesus.

The year prior I'd attended Young Life meetings at the behest of a friend. I knew literally nothing about Jesus before that time—other than his name used as a swear word—and I'd had no idea he had anything to do with Christmas or Easter. So when I heard one of the leaders share the story of Jesus calming the seas (Matthew 8:24-27), I—like the disciples—marveled.

Their question became mine: *Who is this man? Even the winds and waves obey him.*

I listened with rapt attention as the speaker at Camp Timberlake shared about Jesus—his life, the ragtag bunch he hung out with, his pursuit of the broken ones, Judas's betrayal, Jesus' death on a bloodied wooden cross . . . and his shocking resurrection. It all felt like too much, or certainly too good to be true. I was a broken girl, abandoned and alone. Could it really be that Jesus did all that because he loved me and wanted a relationship with the likes of me?

To say that that message rocked me is a beautiful understatement.

I did not speak to anyone as I made my way to the trunk of a giant hemlock, whose heavy branches drooped toward me, as if intent on grabbing me. The stars pinpricked the night under its needled canopy as I sucked in breath, telling myself not to cry. I had been alone and fatherless so long—my biological father had died; my first stepfather had disappeared; my recent stepfather had moved on—and I felt used up, like a dishrag wrung dry.

So I prayed, *Will you be the Father who will never leave me?*

The branches seemed to answer back, no longer menacing. Now the crisp autumn breeze felt like an embrace. All that I had sought through the valley of shadows now became solid—as tangible as the needled earth beneath me. I would be parented. I would be loved. I would not be abandoned. I would (someday) be healed of all this mess. At least that's what I hoped.

That was the day my story pivoted, or at least began the pivot. I was naïve then, believing that the moment I met Jesus meant complete and utter change. In retrospect, the journey toward health and healing was a long slog. A story doesn't change instantly when Jesus enters. He has a lot of long, slow, careful healing work to do in the pages of our lives.

But we do change.

In that wide-eyed bliss of newly knowing Jesus, I would tell myself all was well, that I had already been healed and set free. Mature and hypervigilant, I went on to succeed in school, graduate college with a high GPA, and meet my husband, Patrick, in church—like a good Christian girl. But fissures soon formed in my carefully constructed façade. It all crumbled when my firstborn girl turned five and the sexual trauma resurfaced like a maniacal dragon breathing fire on my carefully curated life. Chronic, unrelenting insomnia; unwanted outbursts of tears; helplessness; and a trauma fog consumed me like thirsty flames.

We could not afford counseling, so I read every book I could find on past abuse, filled out every workbook answer, talked to friends, and sought Jesus for healing—again. It came as slow as molasses as we made our new home far from the Pacific Northwest, where all the pain had happened. I thought I could outrun my story, but it had legs and chased me to the piney woods of East Texas.

But even then, I realized that Jesus was taking me on a restorying adventure of prayer and giving me a longing for a renewed life, healing my broken story, tears upon tears. I went from identifying as a victim to realizing I have been made new. From violated to loved, neglected to wanted, harmed to healed. As I raised my kids in Texas, then France (where Patrick and I served as church planters), God reshaped my self-worth. I no longer felt mired by my past. Through the decades, Jesus used friends, prayer, books, counseling (eventually), and the Bible to bring me to a place of wholeness.

And yet, when God gave me the word *restory*, I had a sense there was more to life than simply being made whole. All that redemption meant something—not merely for me, but for you, too. All that personal wrestling had an endgame. It mattered.

I slowly began to realize this as I listened to a broken friend spilling her story, when I prayed with a new acquaintance at church, when I simply cried with someone. Jesus worked in and through me so that my empathy muscle strengthened. He showed me that the healing he does in our lives is for the sake of us—yes—but also for the flourishing of others. It's for imparting hope in helpless situations, for bringing light to the darkness, for being the hero we longed for when we were younger—for ourselves and for others. We are restoried to help others find their new stories.

Some of the most joyfully profound moments of my life have come on the heels of interceding in the lives of the broken. It's like all that mess finally meant something. Romans 8:28 really is true, friends: "We know that God causes everything [yes, even neglect, divorce, sexual abuse, parental death, and suicidal thoughts] to work together for the good of those who love God and are called according to his purpose for them."

Jesus has a purpose for your pain. He has placed a calling on your life. I know that's hard to comprehend when you're in the middle of a mess. It's not a quick transformation, moving from inward pain toward outward benevolence. And you may think your struggle with the past will never end. That's normal. It's called grief. And lamenting is a necessary practice before breakthrough. Still, the truth remains—God is working through this pathway of pain, making you a blessing to this broken world. You are restoried to bring restoration to your friends, family, and community.

I am a novelist as well as a nonfiction writer, which is to say—I am a storyteller. In the elements of storytelling, we start with the setting, the "normal world" of the story. Good authors explore the time, place, and characters briefly, then something called an inciting incident (yes, seems a bit repetitive, but that's what the English teachers say) bursts onto the scene, followed by the conflicts, rising action, and difficulties. In Western culture, all this mess is followed by a climax, the pinnacle of the story. Only then does the denouement—the working out of the story's climax—occur.

You are currently either approaching or embodying your denouement. And that gets me excited.

Why?

Because your story matters. God will use your story to change lives and alter the landscape of the Kingdom for generations to come. Megachurches, big crowds, and celebrity influence can't do this; Jesus calls us all to work out our stories in the context of close relationships. That's the way he earthquaked our world, upending the way things were—with a gathering of his closest friends. Jesus intersected their stories, restoried them in powerful ways, then encouraged them to be his emissaries of hope in a hopeless world.

Our growth is tied to our stories. Our healing is a narrative discipleship deeply connected to who we are, how God made us, the circumstances surrounding our upbringings, and how we live today in this present world. Our stories evolve over time—and they are profoundly influenced by the people in our lives. The truth is, we don't grow through antiseptic or step-by-step methods, detached from relationships. Human beings are more complicated than that. We need each other as we study the kind of biblical knowledge that transforms us.

This book is my answer to your hunger to let go of what's been holding you back. You no longer need to be enslaved to *back then*, harassed by voices that say you'll never change or get over the pain. If you feel stuck and dissatisfied with how life is unfolding for you and you long to make a difference in this world, it's my prayer that these chapters will help you reframe the difficult story, find healing through Jesus, and begin to grasp the amazing new story he has prepared for you. I'll remine my story to give you footholds in your own so you'll see how God's extraordinary kindness intersects your story. God has uniquely created you and the you-shaped healing journey he has called you to. Your story looks different from your friends' or that leader's. God wants to give you vitality, joy, and effervescent discipleship—the kind that can't help but spill over into this dying world.

So get ready for a journey through your story: the elements and structure and progression of where you have been and who you are becoming. As we look at our lives through the lens of God's restorying process, we'll discover a form, intentionality, and vision for how he's taking what we've thought was only pain or inadequacy and creating something new. Each chapter represents an element of your story, and to put legs to the narrative, we'll also explore the given element through the eyes of a person from Scripture:

- map your own story (Mary of Bethany)
- unearth your setting (Joseph, son of Jacob)
- discover the characters in your story (Peter)
- identify your inciting incidents (Paul)
- endure the muddled middle (the woman with the issue of blood)
- work through your pain points (Job)
- discover the *So what?* of your story (the Ethiopian eunuch)
- walk out your story (Rahab)
- discover the power of your restoried life (the woman at the well)

You'll notice throughout Scripture how God interacts with his people to heal them and bring them new life. Mary of Bethany moved from obscurity to the inner circle of Jesus. Joseph, though betrayed, ended up saving the very ones who had sold him into slavery. Peter shifted from denier of Jesus to a restored, venerated leader in the embryonic church. Paul morphed from a persecutor of Christ followers to considering it a privilege to be persecuted for Jesus. The woman who bled switched from alienation and pain to inclusion and health. Job's story changed from hearing about God to actually seeing him. The Ethiopian eunuch went from not understanding the gospel to being baptized into it. Rahab was an outsider, but she became part of the fabric of Israel—including the lineage of Christ. The woman at the well, a Samaritan, changed from brokenness to wholeness, so much so that she couldn't help but share the love of Jesus with the town that had marginalized her.

The beautiful truth is this: Like the people in the Bible, your growth journey is unique, utterly unique to you. And the Lord will use your personality, gifts, and affections to play an integral part in your discipleship journey. I joke that I've written fifty or so books because I was a mess and God has used every book I've written to bring another facet of healing my way. It's the same for you. God loves you so much that he will use your own unique bent to bring healing your way.

So as you work through this storytelling journey, be expectant. And trust that the Lord does new things all the time—yes, even in and through you.

You may feel like your story is broken.

You may be worried that trauma has negated your ministry potential.

You may be looking at other people's stories with longing, hoping for a different outcome.

You may be discouraged.

You may wonder if you'll ever move beyond your current obstacle.

You may fret that spiritual growth is for others but not for you.

First let me say this: You are normal.

And you bear the image of the almighty God, who loves you, gave himself for you, and is utterly *for* you. No story is insignificant in the Kingdom of God. All are weighted with worth, endowed with purpose, and welcomed as beautiful.

So welcome to your own restoried adventure. May the Lord encircle you, protect your heart, and set you free. Because as you experience all that, you'll become an emancipator of other people's stories—a quiet but necessary revolution and revelation this broken world is crying out for.

Now to him who by the power that is working within us is able to do far beyond all that we ask or think, to him be the glory in the church and in Christ Jesus to all generations, forever and ever. Amen.

EPHESIANS 3:20-21, NET

[illegible] we certai[illegible] [illegible] what's been done [illegible] us [illegible] child, [illegible] may be [illegible] to let [illegible] make [illegible] others [illegible] and the wisdom of [illegible]

Self-editing your [illegible] into [illegible] monster, [illegible]

In short, you may try to [illegible] past [illegible] the [illegible] legs of a [illegible] alien [illegible] you [illegible] with you and [illegible] you, leaving you [illegible] place, [illegible] it. [illegible] your story [illegible] past [illegible] gives you [illegible] heal—and then move on.

The [illegible] these [illegible] different story structures is [illegible] give you [illegible] of a skeleton [illegible] your story upon. It can be [illegible] simple as [illegible] the [illegible] inverted V on a large piece of paper and highlighting pivot points in your life. Just to start off, your birth is the [illegible] moment. You may want to "chunkify" your story [illegible] highlighting the conflicts, traumas, [illegible] relationships that shaped [illegible] decades. The climax [illegible] anything you want—when you [illegible] when you got married, when you had children, or that [illegible] you accomplished last week. There [illegible] a pivot point to your story: a clear before, then after. [illegible] significant traumatic things [illegible] early life. I met Jesus at fifteen, and I've been living in [illegible] working [illegible] to show the results of my salvation, [illegible] with deep reverence and fear" (Philippians [illegible]) [illegible] my restory [illegible] and to be quite honest, [illegible] lifelong journ[illegible]

Or perhaps you relate more to [illegible] journey. In that case, cre[illegible] a circle on a big piece of paper [illegible] words [illegible] in the [illegible] gram. Again, your birth is the [illegible] beginning. Detail who you met along the way, when you [illegible] something differen[illegible] what kind of difficulties and obstacles you faced. Did you have a mome[illegible] of profound change? And what does your life look like now that you've learned so much and you're helping others with their restorying?

The chiastic structure may take a little more thought. What was the main pivot in your life? It could be [illegible]

ONE

Map Your Own Story

Faith never knows where it is being led,
but it loves and knows the One Who is leading.
OSWALD CHAMBERS, *MY UTMOST FOR HIS HIGHEST*

Mary of Bethany

I have always been a girl of many questions—so many that Father often jested that my name was the Questioner. Mother simply scolded my curiosity. But Mother and Father are gone now, dust to dust. I find myself missing their presence.

Now I live in the foothills of Bethany with my dear brother, Lazarus, and my industrious sister, Martha. And still I have questions.

I am aware of the protocols of my religion. As a woman in a world made for men, I cannot ask questions of the local rabbis, nor can I worship fully in the Temple as Lazarus could. But my heart! Oh, my heart longs to know the Almighty, the Rescuer, the One who led the remnant back from captivity. This same God made impossible pathways through a sea and then a river for my people. He vanquished enemies aplenty, reaching from heaven to protect us. He provided a leader in Moses; judges, like Deborah; and kings, like Solomon—all to give us needed guidance and direction. And to worship him? We had a Tabernacle, then a

Temple—a pathway from out to in, from away to welcomed, from alienated to held.

All I have ever wanted has been to know this pathway for myself, to discern the intricate twists and turns of knowing my Creator.

Here is what I know now: The questions and longings from my story have led me toward the hero of my story.

Our family welcomed Jesus, who is called the Christ, into our home. We provided a safe place to stay, offered hospitality, and welcomed him with respite from the dusty roads. Jesus came with twelve companions, who rustled up such appetites that we could scarcely keep them fed. But the "food" Jesus has brought us is what satiates me most.

They say a rabbi's role is to teach, and a student of that rabbi sits at his feet. Oh, how I wanted that place of privilege at the feet of Jesus, whose words were life and breath and hope—pure manna. I would not dare sit in that sacred place—except . . .

There was that moment as Martha bustled around the kitchen and Lazarus laughed among friends . . . and a knowing passed between Jesus and me. I could not hear his beckoning with my ears, but I felt it in my heart—that he would welcome me at his feet, to learn as a student. In that hiccup of time, everything blurred around me. The cacophony of voices faded into warbled music. Preparation of the upcoming meal became an afterthought.

I sat.

I listened.

Jesus spoke.

My heart thrilled.

Before that moment I had been an orphaned sibling, trying to make sense of my longing. But under the steady gaze of Jesus, I found family, community. He, my father and teacher and friend and Lord—and I, his beloved.

Martha's reprimand came, as I expected, and I steadied myself for a rebuke from Jesus' lips, but none came.

Instead?

He smiled. Drew his companions near. Told Martha not to be consumed with details. Then he held my eyes. "There is only one thing worth being concerned about," he said. "Mary has discovered it, and it will not be taken away from her."

I will spend the rest of my life held by those beautiful words.

To be restoried, we must first be *storied*. We must look behind and uncover what once was so that we can discern turning points and the kind of work the Lord wants to do in our lives.

We have a past. We live in the dynamic now. And we have a future.

Unearthing our lifelong story is a daring act. Why? Because though that story can be painful, God is in the midst of every scene, and retelling it to ourselves means we treasure hunt for his ways. As Oswald Chambers notes, God is the leader of our stories.

In recounting our stories, we also help our mental health. Two researchers, Drs. Duke and Fivush, have found that those who know the details of their extended stories have better mental resilience. Did those they studied know what their grandparents did for a living? Did they know how their parents met? "After conducting research on many children and families, and comparing their results to a battery of psychological tests the children had taken, Dr. Duke and Dr. Fivush came to an overwhelming conclusion. The children who knew more about their family's history exhibited far greater control over their lives. They had far greater self-esteem and told a much healthier story to themselves about their family and history."[1]

Friend, uncovering your story—even if the act of doing so scares you—is a gift you give your mental, emotional, and spiritual health. It's brave, but it's also a step toward healing.

The Shape of Your Story

When we keep our stories locked within, when we push them down deep and opt for a façade of normalcy, we don't grow. We certainly don't restory our lives. Instead, we tend to relive what's been done to us. We repeat what we don't process. An untold story, I often tell people, never heals. We see this in generational sins and struggles. If one parent was yelled at as a child, her tendency may be to yell at her kids. But, if she dares to let out her story and make meaning of it through the insight of others and the wisdom of God, she is far more apt to parent differently.

Self-editing your story doesn't eliminate it—it turns it into a monster, screaming to come out in unwanted behavior.

In short, you may try to outrun your past, but it has the tenacious legs of a marathon runner, and it will chase you, catch up with you, and surpass you, leaving you in a fixed place, unable to grow beyond it. Letting out your story knocks the legs out from underneath your past and gives you space to reflect and heal—and then move on.

So how do we best uncover our stories? First, we need to give our stories a shape. Understanding the fundamentals of storytelling across history and cultures can give us a skeleton to hang our stories on.

All storytelling has a shape, a structure—we instinctively know this, whether we're listening to a friend recount a fender bender or reading an ancient myth. As we walk through timeless approaches to storytelling, I want you to be aware of how stories are told. Why? So you can uncover and share your own.

Western Story Structure

Remember the typical story structure I mentioned in the introduction, with the normal story world, an inciting incident, conflicts aplenty, a climax, and a denouement? You may remember this diagram from high school.

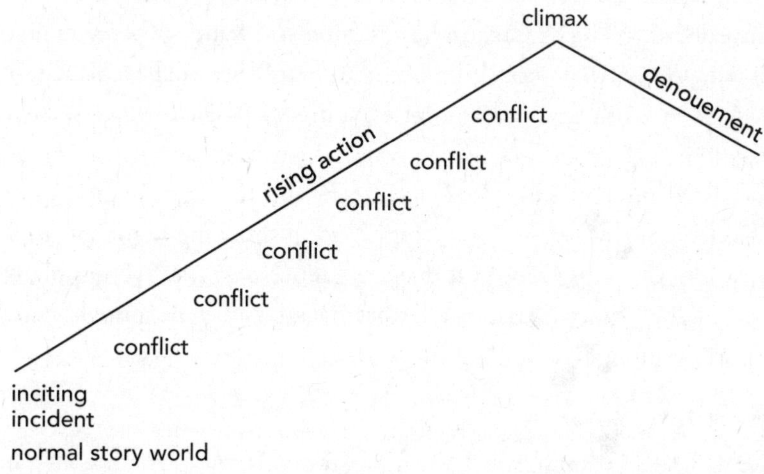

In this format, the story begins in a normal, everyday world when a protagonist is suddenly taken aback by an external (or internal) stressor. A good storyteller then plies the protagonist with conflict upon conflict. Each difficulty, hopefully, holds the reader at rapt attention (or if you're reading a novel, helps you turn the pages deep into the night). When all seems lost, a big hullabaloo happens—the climax—where everything comes to a cataclysmic apex, which is followed by a resolution, also known as the *denouement*, a word we get from French. The protagonist now must learn to live in the new world. In the case of a simple romance, the structure is plain: boy is alone; boy meets girl; all sorts of shenanigans and misunderstandings happen that threaten their burgeoning relationship; a big fight erupts, but they come to a new (happy) understanding; they live happily ever after.

If you want to map out your story in this structure, it can be as simple as drawing the first diagram (the inverted *V*) on a large piece of paper and highlighting pivot points in your life. Just to start you off, your birth is the inciting incident. You may want to "chunkify" your story by taking it in ten-year increments, highlighting what kinds of conflicts, traumas, achievements, and relationships shaped each of those decades. The climax can be anything you want—when you met Christ, got married, had children, or accomplished that accolade last week. There will be a pivot point to your story—a clear *before*, then *after*. For me? From ages one to fifteen, significant traumatic things populated my life. I met Jesus at fifteen, and I've been living in the denouement since then, "work[ing] hard to show the results of [my] salvation, obeying God with deep reverence and fear" (Philippians 2:12). When I met Christ, my restory began, and to be quite honest, I'm still walking out that healing journey.

The Hero's Journey

You're probably familiar with the more in-depth story structure Joseph Campbell maps out in his book *The Hero's Journey*. In the intro to the book, editor Phil Cousineau analyzes the narrative patterns involving a story's hero (protagonist) throughout history, writing, "The journey of the hero is about the courage to seek the depths; the image of creative rebirth; the eternal cycle of change within us; the uncanny discovery that the seeker is the mystery which the seeker seeks to know. The hero journey is a symbol that binds, in the original sense of the word, two distant ideas, the spiritual quest of the ancients with the modern search for identity, 'always the one, shape-shifting yet marvelously constant story that we find.'"[2]

The hero's journey is cyclical, starting in an ordinary world and then quickly becoming an adventure of facing some obstacles, meeting mentors, and despairing of circumstances before finally finding restoration in their story. Here's a rough idea:

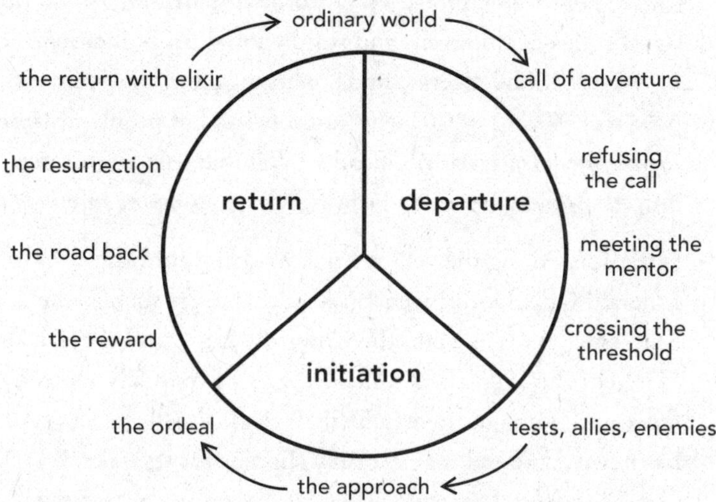

This circle resembles the elements of the three-act structure we see in the first diagram except that the line has been stretched around a curve. The departure represents the very beginning of the journey (the inciting incident and normal story world). The initiation is the rising action with conflict, followed by a dramatic climax. The return is the denouement.

This framework helps us discern the story structure of most of the books we read and movies we consume. Take the 1939 movie *The Wizard of Oz*, for example.

- **Ordinary world.** In the opening scene, Dorothy is in her normal Kansas world, populated by her aunt and uncle, friends, neighbors, and a mean lady on a bike who wants to kill her beloved dog, Toto.
- **Departure.** A tornado turns everything upside down—literally. Dorothy arrives in the magical land of Oz,

inadvertently causing the triumphant defeat of a hated witch (*call of adventure*). However, Dorothy doesn't understand the significance of this event and simply longs for home (*refusing the call*). She meets Glinda, who speaks of the great and powerful Wizard of Oz, who can solve all her problems (*meeting the mentor*). Finally, Dorothy takes that first fateful step onto the yellow brick road toward Oz (*crossing the threshold*).

- **Initiation.** Along the yellow brick road and into the Wizard's Emerald City, Dorothy encounters characters such as the Scarecrow, the Tin Man, the Cowardly Lion, and the Wicked Witch of the West (*tests, allies, enemies*). Eventually Dorothy faces a dilemma in the witch's dark castle—will she let go of her newly acquired magical ruby slippers for the sake of saving Toto's life (*the approach*)? When her friend the Scarecrow is set on fire, Dorothy douses him with water, which dissolves the Wicked Witch (*the ordeal*).

- **Return.** Upon returning to the Emerald City, Dorothy receives a reward—though not in the form we might expect. When Toto removes the curtain of the Wizard of Oz, Dorothy finds him small and certainly not powerful. It's a universal lesson all of us must learn—that those who appear heroic and in control are often simply ordinary people (*the reward*). When the Wizard's hot air balloon accidentally leaves for home without Dorothy, Glinda reappears and tells Dorothy that the ruby slippers can transport her home. Dorothy is the heroine in her own story (*the road back*). Though Dorothy had longed for a life over the rainbow, she is now content to be proactive in her hometown. She awakens in Kansas after a very strange dream, but she is not the same person she was (*the resurrection*). She now has confidence and a deep appreciation for the oft-hidden rewards of home (*the return with elixir*).

We relate to Dorothy, don't we? She is fragile, tenacious, nervous, longing, and at times, heroic. We long for her to win. And as we understand the progression of the hero's journey, we discover our own connections to the overarching story. We can ask ourselves questions like these:

- *When did I meet an important mentor? When didn't I have one but longed for one?*
- *What obstacles have threatened me? What has prevented me from moving forward?*
- *Who has prevented my growth?*
- *What is my calling on this earth, and why is it so hard to fulfill it?*
- *When have I made heroic choices?*
- *What rewards have I experienced along the way?*
- *Do I have enemies? Heroes? Have I gained new insight after trials?*

This story structure leads us to a foundational conclusion: A hero lives an adventure. A hero makes choices, often hard ones. A hero faces difficulties and overcomes them. And if we are the heroes of our own stories in a sense, this kind of purposeful action is necessary. We always have a choice, no matter how random the conflicts we face or how uprooted our lives currently feel.

If the hero's journey feels resonant as you look at your own story, create a circle on a big piece of paper with the words I've shared in the diagram. Again, your birth is the normal story world's beginning. Detail when you've felt the call to something different, whom you've met along the way, what kinds of difficulties and obstacles you've faced. Have you had a moment of profound change? And what does your life look like now that you've learned so much and you're helping others with their restorying?

The Chiasm

As I was writing this chapter, a reader shared this painful story with me:

> My sweet dog had been anxious during the night in the wake of a storm that sat over our home for several hours. I was up with her, and then, when daylight came, we went outside to explore before anyone else woke up. In one corner of our backyard, there was a new light shining through where hours before the shade of a beautiful oak tree had graced and anchored the space. A massive tree had been *yanked* from the ground in the storm overnight.
>
> What I saw there looked so much like what had happened to me ten years earlier—everything uprooted, my life yanked out of all that felt grounded and secure—even though deep down I had known there were problems. I was in an unhealthy church serving an abusive pastor, and I had prayed for God's rescue, but wow, I didn't see it going that way. I had loved that part of my life in so many ways. It was brutal to lose it. And I loved this tree in my backyard. It brought covering and shade and what felt like protection. And now it's gone—or more accurately, it's in pieces on the ground . . . all of the goodness lost, which is such grief. All of the pieces on the ground, so disorienting and strange. And now, new light seeping through where the leaves once caught shadows.[3]

The reader, Connie, viewed this fallen tree through the lens of story. She welcomed it as a metaphor for a time of crushing and new life—where light can stream through what had been torn down. God is so good to open our eyes to the story he is unfolding around us, isn't he?

Connie probably didn't realize it, but her story takes on an even more ancient story structure—that of chiasm, which emerges from ancient Near Eastern literature. The Bible is full of chiasm, where the climax of the story isn't at the end but lies in its belly, between the opening story element and a corresponding element at the end. Because the Bible wasn't written with italicized or bolded text, this literary device helped readers discover the most important piece of a story immediately.

The word *chiasm* (or *chiasmus*) has to do with the Greek letter *chi*, which resembles the letter *X*. There is a point in the story where everything changes, a hinge between what comes before and its echo afterward.

Old Testament professor Robert J. Chisholm Jr. explains, "A more sophisticated and elaborate form of delimitation involves the use of *chiasmus*, where the themes or key words of the first half of a literary unit are mirrored in the second half. Often a pivotal element is highlighted by its central position in such a structure. Once the cycle of elements has come full circle, the reader (in the original context, the listener) senses the unit is complete."[4]

Once you understand the nature of the structure, you won't be able to unsee it as you study your Bible. Here's what it looks like:

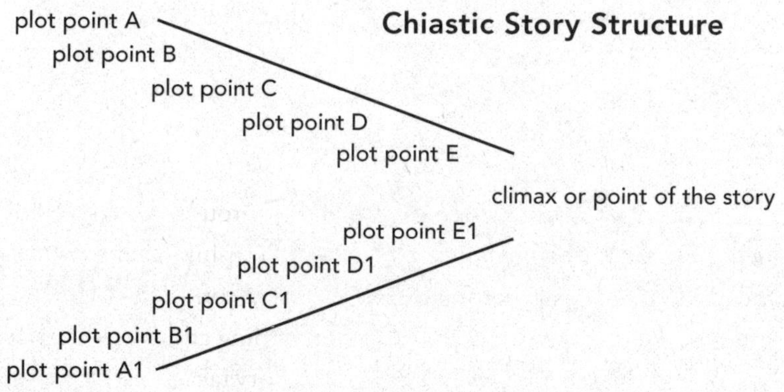

I'll make it simple for you, putting a bit of meat on the bones of this structure using John 4:23-24.

The time is coming—indeed it's here now—when true worshipers *will worship the Father in spirit and in truth.*

The Father is looking for those who will *worship him* that way.

For God is Spirit,

so those who *worship him*

must worship *in spirit and in truth.*

The central part of the chiasm, "For God is Spirit," is the fulcrum of the passage. Notice how the first part and last part directly correspond to each other, repeating *worship* and *spirit* and *truth*. The middle part's repetition is "worship him."

Looking at Connie's story, we see the light pushing through her backyard as the central point of the story. Prior to that, a storm, then the felling of the tree. She then recounts her painful church story as a storm, then destruction, which led to new light in a new place.

storm

felling of tree

new light

felling of her church

church storm

As you map out your own story, the chiastic structure may take a little more thought. What was the main pivot in your life? It could be a decision to stop drinking or the moment of salvation or the time you walked away from that abusive relationship. Now look to see what earlier events correspond to your more current events. What patterns do you notice? What story are you trying to complete?

Here's something I've spotted in mine. Two predators found me at five—and later a Christian-publishing professional preyed on me in my late thirties. Obviously the instances differed widely, and I hope I had more tools to deal with the second occurrence, but they did happen. In the time between those two predations, I met Jesus, who began to heal me—the main pivot point in my life.

As I started to look at these events through the structure of a chiastic story, one thing became very clear to me. My first abusers were predators, and they were narcissistic. The man in the publishing industry was a predatory narcissist. Stepping back to look at other pieces of my story, I kept noticing that I even pursued female friends who fit that mold as well. And I had family members who were either predators or narcissists.

I realized that this was the story I was trying to complete: If I could prove a predatory narcissist liked me, I could prove my lovability to those in my family of origin who had treated me with contempt, dismissal, or predation. Since my earlier family hadn't completed my story with love, I spent many years as an adult pursuing unsafe people, hoping desperately that they could complete my story. The problem was that predators and/or narcissistic people make very poor saviors. They are so busy using others that the last thing on their minds is how to salve a broken person's wound.

Understanding the pattern in those stories, I finally realized I was going about things all wrong. I would keep living my past story if I didn't go to Jesus to finish my story. I'd keep circling the drain, hoping I wouldn't fall in the trap. Without healing, my chiasm would play on repeat.

I am now far more aware when I run into folks who exhibit predatory or narcissistic traits. I remind myself that I am loved and sufficient and don't need their approval, validation, or love to feel okay about myself. I am loved by the One who died for me, and that is enough. This realization has helped me stop a painful cycle.

If the way I'm writing about this realization sounds easy or antiseptic, know that the journey here was neither. It took many years of chasing after unsafe people (hoping against hope that they'd suddenly change into trustworthy folks) and getting burned and hurt too many times to count before I had the *aha* about what I was doing. By going to counseling, processing with my husband and friends, and learning what traits safe people possess, I slowly worked through the why of my mess. To be honest, predatory people and narcissists still hold sway over me. Perhaps they always will. The difference is that I am more aware.

That's the power of mapping your story.

You're Not Alone

God's best work is done when he intersects with our most difficult experiences. His kindness is beautifully available, particularly when you're weakened or fearful.

In Isaiah 63:9 we are reminded of God's great compassion toward us, even when it's hard to personally process our grief:

> In all their suffering he also suffered,
>   and he personally rescued them.
> In his love and mercy he redeemed them.
>   He lifted them up and carried them
>   through all the years.

God had powerfully delivered the nation of Israel from Egyptian slavery and led them through their wilderness wanderings and into the Promised Land. But the Israelites did not heed the warnings of the Lord, who loved and led them—instead of worshiping him, they abandoned him to serve idols. That idolatry led to their exile in Babylon. This verse was addressed to that group of exiled people—the remnant, who may have been feeling that God had abandoned them. But here we see God's great mercy toward those he loves.

He has that same heart toward you, friend.

You have walked a similar path. Before you knew Jesus, you were enslaved to sin, brokenhearted and wayward. Jesus rescued you by sacrificing himself on a cross and resurrecting on day three. He literally fought the foe of death and sin on your behalf. As a Christ follower, perhaps you've been prone to wander—an achingly difficult part of your story. Even so, your Lord has affection toward you. He does not despise your story, even if it's full of bumps and bruises and foibles and regrets. He will lift you up and carry you when you don't feel worthy of love or attention.

And the good news is this: He already knows your entire story. In fact, he knows it better than you do. He "formed you in your mother's womb" (Jeremiah 1:5). He created your "once upon a time," and he knows your last breath. He delights in giving wisdom to those he loves—particularly about how to navigate next steps in a difficult story.

If you feel nervous or fearful about looking more closely at your story, know that your compassionate Father is with you every step of the way, just as he was with his people even in their rebellion and wanderings. And he wants you to be honest. He knows that untruth causes pain and hiding but that authenticity brings us into the light. We must mine our stories, not to wallow in them or stay tethered to them in unhealthy ways that leave us stuck, but to learn from them.

Once we're willing to truly face our stories alongside God, we begin the restory process—but we don't do that alone. Our relational God intends for our healing to happen in relationship with others. Telling our stories invites other people into community. Every time each one of us is bold enough to honestly share our story with others, the story lessens, its bite weakens, and we experience a surprising bonus: We make friends. When my husband and I left our megachurch of twenty-three years, we joined a small local church. My husband began attending a weekly meeting of men in the church who simply told their stories. A few weeks into the series, they invited him to share his story. In that moment, he felt welcomed home. Now whenever we attend this new church, Patrick is greeted by new friends. Like you, his story is full of ups and downs—but the sheer act of sharing it vulnerably opened his life up to new friendships.

As I've been praying my way through the writing of this book, I've been asking the Lord for a passage of Scripture to serve as an anchor for the principles herein. Hebrews 12:1-4 has kept coming to mind. Why? Because it mentions community and Jesus' compassion—two important elements in telling our stories.

> Since we are surrounded by such a huge crowd of witnesses to the life of faith, let us strip off every weight that slows us down, especially the sin that so easily trips us up. And let us run with endurance the race God has set before us. We do this by keeping our eyes on Jesus, the champion who initiates and perfects our faith. Because of the joy awaiting him, he endured the cross, disregarding its shame. Now he is seated in the place of honor beside God's throne. Think of all the hostility he endured from sinful people; then you won't become weary and give up. After all, you have not yet given your lives in your struggle against sin.
>
> HEBREWS 12:1-4

The Lord surrounds us with a cloud of witnesses, both in the heavens *and* in the earthly realm. We are called to live out our stories with verve and intention. Jesus is our goal, but he is also our means of walking with integrity and hope. Why? Because he endured all things for our sake. He is a merciful friend who has experienced the hell of this life—and he knows best how to intersect and heal our stories.

My challenge to you before you move on to the next chapter, with Jesus as your companion, is to map your journey using one of the frameworks I shared earlier. There is no teacher grading your effort; it can look however you want—a story arc, a hero's circle, a chiasm, a song, a drawing, a poem, a recounting by voice into your phone. These tools I'm offering you are simply frameworks to get everything out onto the page (or into the microphone and transcribed). And since each one is a diagram, that can eliminate the fear of writing a very, very long essay about your life. You can write fragments in the margins—or one word to remind you of that time when you were eleven. You can draw a picture if that best fits the way you remember your past. The point is to get it out—at least for your sake. If you fear the reactions of others, I encourage you to show your diagram or written-out story with a safe friend. All you need to do is slide the paper across the table and let them see it. In that shared space, you are no longer bearing your story alone. That place of safe community, then, becomes the first step of the restorying process.

Restorying Mary of Bethany

As you pull this together, I want you to watch closely for ways the Lord has intersected your story, similarly to the way I imagined Mary of Bethany at the top of this chapter. How did he rescue you? When did he seem aloof? When were you discouraged? What people have helped you? What people have served as adversaries? What themes have emerged? Can you see a thread of redemption—or of struggle or patterns of relating that you'd like to change?

To be restoried is to let out your story first—it's to give it weight and dignity. And it means you must learn self-compassion. Be kind to little you back then. Take off your hat of judgment and choose to offer mercy to the child who was just trying to make it in the world. If you remember something differently than your sibling does, that's normal and okay. Every person you meet sees the world through a different lens. That doesn't make one story correct and another wrong; it simply means we live in a world of nuance. Maybe your parents' harsh treatment of you really affected you while your sister felt it was what she needed to help her achieve things. We all experience our families of origin differently—and that makes sense. This happened at the beginning of time with Cain and Abel. They didn't experience their parents in the same way, nor did they interact with God in the same way.

You have permission to own your story. You are allowed to tell it however you would like to. Pray that the Lord will give you insight and direction as you work through your timeline. And be prepared for healing and change.

Telling your story is an audacious step toward a restoried life. I'm so proud of you for taking this journey.

Questions for Discussion

1. Which story structure was the most familiar to you? The least?
2. How does understanding different ways of telling a story help you share your own?
3. How does Mary of Bethany's story teach you about telling your own?
4. When have you finally let out a story to a trusted person, and how did you feel after you shared it?
5. How difficult was it for you to recount your story the first time?

[illegible] when we push th[illegible]

down deep [illegible] grow. We certa[illegible] [illegible] done [illegible] us [illegible] children [illegible] to let others' story and take meaning [illegible] others, and the wisdom of God [illegible]

Self-editing your [illegible]

monster, [illegible]

Instead, you may try to [illegible] past, [illegible] legs of a marathon. [illegible] you and surprises you, leaving you [illegible] place, unable to move beyond it. Letting out your stories [illegible] out from under [illegible] past and gives you space to reflect and heal—and then move on.

The rest [illegible] different story structures [illegible] give you [illegible] of a skeleton to hang your story upon. It [illegible] simple as drawing the first diagram (the inverted V) on a [illegible] of paper and marking [illegible] points in your life. Just to start off your [illegible] you may want to quickly [illegible] highlighting the points, traumas, [illegible] relationships that [illegible] decades. The [illegible] can be anything you want—when you [illegible] when you got married, when you had children, or that accomp[illegible] you accomplished at work. There will be a pivot point to your story [illegible] before, then after. For me, [illegible] one to fifteen [illegible] traumatic [illegible] early life. Then Jesus [illegible] fifteen, and I've been living in the aftermath since then, working hard to show the results [illegible] reverence and fear" [illegible] story [illegible] and to be quite honest, [illegible]

Or perhaps you [illegible] case, [illegible] a circle [illegible] I've engaged in the [illegible] again, your circle is the story from its beginning. Detail wh[illegible] you met along the way, when you felt the call to something differe[illegible] what kind of difficulties and sorrows you faced. Did you have a mom[illegible] of profound change? And what does your life look like now that you've learned so much and you're helping others with their restorying?

The chiastic structure may take a little more thought. What wa[illegible]

TWO

Unearth Your Setting

The most important element in fostering a sense of place is to teach ourselves, or let ourselves be taught, to see with fresh eyes the place where we find ourselves. . . . It is a great and worthy effort, and few objectives could be more conducive to the common good.

WILFRED M. McCLAY, "THE SPACE WAS OURS BEFORE WE WERE THE PLACE'S," IN *WHY PLACE MATTERS*

Joseph, Son of Jacob

From where I sit now, it is easy enough to gloss over the pain. After all, I am viceroy over the entirety of Egypt; my brothers and fathers have resettled in Goshen; our people are preserved and thriving. But the place we live now is certainly not the place I long for when I stare up at the stars dotting the sky. Yes, yes, the stars appear the same in Egypt as they do in Canaan, but I can't help but think they shine brighter there. My bones long for the place of my birth—the halcyon days before the troubles.

Looking back, I can see that the coat Father gave me began the enmity between my brothers and me, although, as I think about it, perhaps my youthful dream boasting mortared it into place. And so, when Father sent me to check on them, my fate unraveled. Hearing my brothers' voices plot, being sent tumbling into the belly of the earth, listening from the desolate pit as they wagered and sold me as chattel—these are the memories that haunt me. In one horrid moment, I lost my family, my dreams, my coat, my home, my life.

I remember the scent of my mother as she prepared lamb. The grit of the soil beneath our tent. The jesting of my brothers on the open plain. The roughness of Father's beard. Home meant everything to me. As I busied myself under the rule of Potiphar, in a home so different from my own, I strained to hold on to my memories. The contrast fueled my longing for return.

But return never came.

I still knew that my ultimate master was the Lord God Almighty, so when Potiphar's wife tried to entrap me, I fled—though it did me no good. In a swift moment, just as quick as my brothers' decision, I was plunged once more into the earth, this time into Pharaoh's dank prison—the kind of place that drips musty and houses the "deserving."

But then my penchant for dream interpretation resparked. A baker. A cupbearer. Both burdened by dreams that either saved or destroyed them. The one who was saved promised to remember me, but again I was forgotten. I asked God to spare me, to see me, to rescue me, but the heaven I could not see fell silent.

Until.

I was summoned from the underworld, shaved, bathed, and reclothed—called to see the most powerful man in the land of Egypt. Under the shadow of pyramids and the Sphinx, he tasked me with the impossible: to interpret catastrophic dreams. I told him, of course, that I had no skills in this area, that only God could do such a miracle—and, by the hesed of God, the interpretation flowed from me: abundance for seven years followed by the worst sort of famine.

The land we lived in, the land that had swallowed me in a dungeon, would betray Pharaoh eventually. But a solution formed in my mind—grain storehouses full to the brim to stave off starvation.

And then came the day my brother-betrayers bowed before me—a dream come true in the oddest sense—and begged for help. My insides roiled at the sight of them. Time had made my heart tender toward them, but the pain remained. Here I stood, slave exile turned royalty, fighting tears and longing for home. No matter how much betrayal one experiences, isn't there always that animal need for the familiar? The scents, the sounds, the cadence of life in a nearly forgotten place called home?

Once the truth was revealed, the reconciliation came, and even Father was in my embrace. The broken part of me felt nearly whole. The rejoicing reverberated through me. I once was dead to Father, but now I lived before him in a foreign land. I returned the favor of life—he and Mother gave it to me, and now I measured it back in abundance, a holy privilege.

Even so, I asked that my bones be returned home. One day.

How do you restory a place?

How does God redeem a setting?

I have spent many hours walking through places in my mind, trying to mine their meaning. Perhaps it's just the way my brain works, but I associate nearly every memory not with a smell or what I heard while there but with what the walls looked like or how the sun shone at a particular angle. I remember my life in snapshots, perhaps because my biological father was a black-and-white photographer. Remnants of his aperture hide in eight-by-ten-inch boxes in my closet, photos of places I still remember, though sometimes I strain to do so.

My traumatic fifth year shows up in a snapshot of the cracked sidewalk leading to the tiny white house with paint so peeled that it appeared like driftwood in color. My black cats stretch out on the porch hammock, gently swaying beneath an impossibly blue Seattle sky. Alki Beach looms a few scant blocks away, and the taste of salt lingers in the Puget Sound air. Inside the house, a grow closet boasts healthy, leafy marijuana plants.

I don't remember eating a meal in that house, but my fear of not having enough food certainly originated within its crooked walls. I created my own version of home in an attached shed that housed our gas and water meters, complete with cached Halloween candy just in case I got hungry.

Not far from that house sat Eva's home—my babysitter's place. Her house seemed haunted, painted dirt gray and smelling of cigarettes. There were other children in her home, but I have no memory of them. Perhaps that's because a five-year-old only has the capacity to carry one big memory.

The boys who lived next door to Eva stole me away to terrifying woods and other dark corners of our neighborhood, and these few square blocks of modest, beachy homes became the setting of some of the worst trauma of my life. I could not return there until several decades had passed, and even then, my cavalier feeling of triumph could not forestall the involuntary vomiting that followed.

Our bodies remember[1]—even when we spout off platitudes about Jesus rescuing and healing us. I fully felt healed, but my stomach betrayed me on a grand scale.

That place? It was haunted.

That setting? The stage for betrayal and predation.

Honestly? I never want to return.

How do we work through the settings of our stories? How can we find Jesus in those places that remain menacing years after the danger has passed? Should we simply avoid them? Stop thinking of them? And what do we make of places that once seemed idyllic but that have shape-shifted after years of understanding? I remember my husband telling me he had a perfect childhood with doting, kind parents. This was true on one level. But as he grew older, and when he had children, he began to see the past with new eyes. He started remembering interactions that had been less than helpful, some bordering on neglectful. His story changed, in a way, as he reflected on the settings of his life with adult eyes.

Has that happened to you? Have you ever held one belief about the past only to come to the stark realization that life was different from what you first perceived?

An exploration of the *where* of where you came from is an important part of your restory journey. Whether you mentally walk through all your old homes as I do or you can barely remember your bedroom from when you were seven, I believe exploring the setting of your story will unlock insights into how you interact with the world today.

Here are some of the ways *Merriam-Webster* defines *setting*:

> a: the time, place, and circumstances in which something occurs or develops
> b: the time and place of the action of a literary, dramatic, or cinematic work
> c: the scenery used in a theatrical or film production.[2]

Friend, you are a cinematic work, and your setting matters. Where you have been has influenced who you are today—just as it did in the life of Joseph, who was deeply tied to his place as one of twelve sons of Jacob. And much of what he experienced later corresponded to his homeland. He was injured in one locale and then healed in another.

The memory of place matters, yes, but so does the place you inhabit today. I've experienced the redemption of a past place of hurt in the soil of a current place of provision and safety—similar to Joseph. In a new place, with his newfound position of prominence and leadership, he could forgive his family, pursue reconciliation, and experience radical restoration.

My husband recently reminded me of an important biblical principle related to place and setting: that not letting their land have a Sabbath rest was one of the reasons the Israelites were sent into exile. We see this play out in Leviticus 26:33-35, when God warns, "I will scatter you among the nations and bring out my sword against you. Your land will become desolate, and your cities will lie in ruins. Then at last the land will enjoy its neglected Sabbath years as it lies desolate while you are in exile in the land of your enemies. Then the land will finally rest and enjoy the Sabbaths it missed. As long as the land lies in ruins, it will enjoy the rest you never allowed it to take every seventh year while you lived in it."

God's intention was for the Israelites to so fully rely on him that they would allow the land to lie fallow every seventh year. But they didn't. And God reminds them in this passage that trusting in themselves and worshiping at the altar of control would have consequences.

We see this in our own lives when we cease from resting. Overworking, overstressing, and overscheduling inevitably end up sidelining us. Nights without sleep end with days of sleeping as we battle sickness. We will rest one way or another—but only when we intentionally pursue rest will we find soul health. It's always better to choose rest than be forced to succumb to it.

For those of us who want to restory our settings, sometimes sabbathing means walking away from a place for a period of time to heal. When we carry a deep wound, going back to a painful place can be like exposing it to further infection. We may need to walk away from a setting to heal without the environment causing old traumas to fester.

Only when I moved away from the Seattle area to East Texas in my thirties did I have enough editorial distance to really see what had happened to me and how my setting had contributed to further trauma. Once I stopped swimming in that environment and stood at a distance, I could spy out the land more keenly and begin to see how much healing I needed.

I would not be where I am today had I not trekked across the country. A further move to the land of France gave me even more distance. Part of the reason moving helped was that I no longer had crutches or familiar footholds. In an unknown environment where I felt out of sorts, I was more apt to rely on the Lord. I had to make him my place of safety. I familiarized myself with Psalms like these:

> I love you, LORD;
>   you are my strength.
> The LORD is my rock, my fortress, and my savior;
>   my God is my rock, in whom I find protection.
> He is my shield, the power that saves me,
>   and my place of safety.
>
> PSALM 18:1-2

> You are my hiding place;
>   you protect me from trouble.
>   You surround me with songs of victory.
>
> PSALM 32:7

> As for me, I will sing about your power.
>   Each morning I will sing with joy about your unfailing love.
> For you have been my refuge,
>   a place of safety when I am in distress.
>
> PSALM 59:16

Those who live in the shelter of the Most High
will find rest in the shadow of the Almighty.
This I declare about the LORD:
He alone is my refuge, my place of safety;
he is my God, and I trust him.

PSALM 91:1-2

In places unfamiliar, I learned through experience that only God could be my setting of *shalom*. He became my resting place. He was the hiding place I ran to when life overwhelmed me.

Benjamin Hardy, the author of *Willpower Doesn't Work*, elaborates on the importance of changing your setting: "When you expose yourself to new ideas, new experiences, or things you've long feared, you will have what social scientists call a *disorienting dilemma*. This often occurs when people travel to foreign countries, but it can even happen by doing activities you've never done before. A disorienting dilemma is when your current mental model is somewhat shattered through exposure to new ideas or experiences that contradict your current way of thinking."[3]

Moving away or taking a step back helps you reframe everything, and it may empower you to get closer to your breakthrough.

Does this mean you have to pull up stakes and move away from your home of origin?

No.

But you can use your times of travel, seasons when you're out of your typical environment, to ask the Lord to bring deeper and further healing. Often our vacations are so packed with activities that we need long periods of rest afterward. But what if we viewed our travels as an opportunity to sabbath? What if, as we remember the story of Joseph, we understand that much of his healing happened away from home? And what would have happened to the Israelites had they given their land rest and not worshiped idols? God's unique plan for all of us includes the command to keep the Sabbath holy, to rest in a weekly rhythm—not to bother us but to heal us. We neglect rest to our peril. And often we need rest from our places of trauma.

Finding Safety

Sometimes God calls us to return to our settings (like he did for me with the little white house) to face what happened there. Be forewarned though. According to the groundbreaking book *The Body Keeps the Score*, by Bessel van der Kolk, trauma lives in our bodies.[4] Don't be surprised if your mind feels fine to visit that place of violation but your body rejects it. Be gentle with yourself. Provide ways of escape or retreat if you feel your stomach roil or you become lightheaded.

While I did experience those symptoms when I revisited the place of my multiple sexual assaults, they didn't reoccur when my eldest daughter and I returned to southern France, where both of us (along with the rest of our family) had endured much trauma. We were both surprised at how well we did (maybe because we got to eat pain au chocolat whenever we felt sad). We prayed in front of my daughter's international school. We took an excursion to an enchanting island to give ourselves a new, fun memory. And we had conversations with people who brought life-giving insight into our time in France. As my husband, Patrick, reminded me, we had unknowingly been paratroopers in a spiritual war when we'd moved to France with our family. We'd parachuted behind enemy lines and had gigantic targets on our family. We'd suffered in nearly every way imaginable—financially, emotionally, physically, mentally, relationally, spiritually. And it took us leaving France and coming back home to begin to restory that time in our lives. We had to heal in a safe place.

Part of restorying our settings—keep in mind that a setting is made up of people—is to understand what a safe place is. Some of us have spent so many years in unsafe environments that we cannot discern what is good and kind and safe. To find safe places to heal, you can identify signs of healthy boundaries, respect, and care. Here are some footholds to help you uncover the traits of safe settings.[5]

Safe Settings Give You Space

Sometimes our stories are too heavy and we need space to process. Safe settings understand this. They don't take your need for space personally or pressure you to explain. Instead, safe settings allow you the time needed to process, supporting you in silence, knowing that sometimes the best way to show up is to step back. Safe settings don't demand your blind servitude, don't shame you for pulling back, and empathize when you're not at capacity. They allow you to live your story and don't try to form you into theirs. The people in the system or setting don't use language like *Whatever it takes* or *It's my way or the highway*. A safe setting allows you to pull away, regroup, and rejoin.

Safe Settings Have Your Back

A safe setting allows for people to step in and defend you with kindness and strength when you're maligned. They don't expose your vulnerabilities or belittle you when you're walking through pain. Instead, they become your shield, ensuring you feel supported and valued. A safe setting creates a protective layer between you and the harsh world. It's a haven. I've often longed to create a haven-like home for my kids, a place they'd be wildly enthusiastic about coming back to after their time at school. Sadly, few of us have experienced a haven, a shelter, a place where we're protected. Perhaps that's why there is so much language in the Bible referring to the importance of having a Good Shepherd. Shepherds protect sheep—they provide a haven.

Safe Settings Assume Positive Intent

We have all experienced the pain of misunderstanding. It's particularly egregious when our motives are slandered unfairly. In an unsafe setting, people jump to negative conclusions about you immediately, without any clarification. Many families fit this broken model of always assuming the worst. You cannot thrive if someone (or a group of someones) constantly disparages you and assigns nefarious motives to you. In contrast, people in safe settings ask if everything is all right, believing your good intentions and giving grace.

Recently a pastor reached out to me because he heard I had said something negative about him in the media. Thankfully, he said he'd assumed that it couldn't be true, but he wanted to find out what I did say. We worked out the issue, and I was able to reassure him that the rumor was untrue. I thanked him for assuming the best about me—it made me feel safe.

Safe Settings Let You Be You

Your quirks, your passions, your unique way of navigating life—these traits are celebrated in a safe setting. A safe environment doesn't try to mold you into someone else or force you into the culture's ideal. There's also little envy in a safe setting. Everyone celebrates one another's uniqueness, choosing not to be intimidated by the giftings of others. We must remember that everyone's setting is unique—we all carry the scars and badges from our upbringings, and we all have differing lenses through which we see the world. In the new church we are attending, I'm really enjoying just being me without even being attached to my vocation. People are getting to know me just for me, and there is freedom in that.

Safe Settings Speak the Truth but in Love

Life-giving systems care about your well-being. If you're making choices that may hurt you, people in a safe system will gently point out the potential harm but with kindness, self-awareness, and deep care for you as a person. They do this *not* to harshly judge you but to support your growth, always being willing to help you find your way back to a healing path. Unsafe settings can err either way—by stating the truth harshly and with malice or by avoiding saying anything because it's uncomfortable. The apostle Paul puts it well: "We will speak the truth in love, growing in every way more and more like Christ, who is the head of his body, the church" (Ephesians 4:15).

Safe Settings Welcome the Truth but Without Gossiping

Finding systems with people who respect your words is gold. Safe settings don't give in to gossip; they don't betray things spoken in confidence. Your story remains safe with them, and they won't speak ill of you when you're not around. Proverbs 25:9-10 reminds us, "When arguing with your neighbor, / don't betray another person's secret. / Others may accuse you of gossip, / and you will never regain your good reputation." People in safe settings love to protect your reputation.

Safe Settings Don't Demand Trust

People in safe settings respect your boundaries and your no. They don't just love your yes. They also don't demand blind trust just because they may be in authority over you. Instead, they win your trust by behaving in a trustworthy manner. Whenever a system demands blind obedience, reevaluate—you may be in an unsafe, cultic place. While it is important to respect people, that respect doesn't need to continue if the person demanding it becomes abusive.

Safe Settings Welcome Your Growth

Sometimes people or systems only see you for what you used to be and cannot conceive of your growth or understand that you've moved beyond who you were back then. One of my family members thought of me as the shy girl who never spoke up. She'd been categorizing me as reticent ever since she got that impression, not realizing how much I had grown in reaching out to people, making friends, and navigating complex work and ministry situations. While the fact that I tended to retract may have been true at the time (when I was living traumatized), it is not true of me now.

Growth is a natural part of life. Safe environments embrace this truth. A safe group of friends celebrates your progress. They don't feel threatened or left behind when you grow beyond them. A safe setting takes notice, praises your tenacity, views your growth favorably, and applauds it.

Safe Settings Don't Demand Conformity

To be in a system that demands conformity is to decolor our world. These days we've become so accustomed to siloing ourselves, only befriending people with similar views to ours, that we're missing out on the richness of good conversation. The beauty of life erupts from diversity. People in safe settings value your differences and the unique way you better the environment. Whether you're outspoken or quiet or have different political opinions from the people around you, your distinctions improve your setting. Think of a safe setting as an interesting dinner party with a wide variety of guests. Over a meal you learn a lot about the world because everyone there shares their ideas.

Safe Settings Don't Shame

Shame often plays a painful role as you look back on unsafe places. No one can thrive in a shame-based setting. If you live in one, you will constantly be looking over your shoulder, second-guessing yourself, wondering when you're going to get in trouble again. People in safe systems never make you feel small or broken. They accept you, with your flaws and quirks, without constantly hammering you about your shortcomings. A safe setting is a place where you have freedom—freedom to be yourself, freedom to fail and rise back up, freedom to restory your life.

Many times in my life I have despaired of settings. A few years ago, I spoke up against sexual abuse and how it's handled in SBC (Southern Baptist Convention) churches. I spent myself for that broken system only to see the leadership backpedal, preferring reputation management over a harder but more authentic process of restorying the narrative. To be honest, I've let that time in my life wound me, and I'm still trying to crawl out of the cynicism. I've learned that I'm just no good at politics and trying to change entrenched systems. Perhaps that's why the apostle Paul uses the language he uses when he talks about spiritual warfare: "We are not fighting against flesh-and-blood enemies, but against evil rulers and authorities of the unseen world, against mighty powers in this dark world, and against evil spirits in the heavenly places" (Ephesians 6:12). These demonic powers influence systems, and those systems don't easily give up power. They can strangle dissent while keeping their influence and reputations as the most important things. Breaking free from settings like this involves a cataclysmic shift. In researching cultic and/or narcissistic systems, I've found that we can swim in an environment for so long that we believe being treated in an unsafe way is normal and good. It's only when we change settings that our eyes are opened to what we've walked through—and then our eyes cannot help but stay open.

Have you ever had that happen to you? Maybe you were being harmed in a group or family or job or ministry and you hung on, feeling like something was not quite right but not being able to put your finger on it. But then eventually you realized it was not a safe or healthy place, and you took a tentative step away. Once you fully walked away, you suddenly became far more capable of seeing the dissension, shame, and painful ways of relating. It became apparent. In that new space, you could not unsee the dysfunction.

That doesn't mean you don't eventually work for reconciliation. But in that tender space of moving away, you may need to take some time to heal before you dive back into a difficult setting. Be kind to yourself. Take note of your bodily reactions. Ask friends or a counselor to help you assess when you're ready.

Restorying Joseph

The woman's words shouted through my phone while I sat at the old oak round table that had been gifted to me by my mother's boyfriend. That antique with its solid base was, to me, stability, and it had followed my family around the world from Seattle to Palestine, Texas, to outside Nice, France, and back to North Texas. I steadied myself there as her angry voice flung accusation after accusation, assigning horrible motives to me that were untrue.

The rise of her voice sent me reeling back to my first-grade classroom, where the teacher had scolded me for doing something I thought had been good but had then discovered had ruined something unintentionally. My heart rate now echoed that of six-year-old me as I "got in trouble."

In instances like these, when I'm attacked, my response is not to fight back or to flee. I typically freeze and then fawn.[6] For a long time I allowed the woman's voice to gain momentum as I sat at the oak table, silent. And then I fawned, backed down, and clicked off the phone. Elbows to oak, I wept at my little round table. I had been abused quite intensely for a few months by this woman. The caustic phone call was, thankfully, the goodbye to all that.

All at once, when the tears stopped, peace flowed over me. God had set me free from this untenable situation. I still existed in the same setting, but I had been emancipated.

It's funny how a setting can shift.

So, too, when we look at Joseph's story, we see a restory of his setting, though he never did fully return to his homeland—except as a skeleton. Yet his very existence and tenacity preserved his people so that one day they would be alive to enter the Promised Land. Joseph had been robed by God with blessing, was robbed through testing, and became robust by entrusting himself to the Lord in his exilic state. Look at the actions he experienced in various locales. Joseph was

1. mocked,
2. abandoned,
3. exploited,
4. betrayed,
5. misunderstood,
6. maligned,
7. imprisoned, and
8. forgotten.

Do you see yourself in these words? Have these terms or actions populated the setting of your story? Look back over your past year. When have you been mocked? Has someone abandoned you to face something difficult purely on your own? Have you felt exploited or used? Has someone betrayed your trust? Has someone (or a group) chosen to assign wrong motives to you and deeply misunderstood your heart? Have you been maligned, privately or publicly? Many will not have faced imprisonment as Joseph did, but we do sometimes live in metaphorical prisons of others' making (and even our own—a prison of fear, for example). Have you felt the sting of being forgotten?

All these elements of a difficult story rest in conflict, and conflicts are often tied to a setting.

But while Joseph experienced the pain of these eight offenses, the settings of his life were restoried into eight beautiful truths. I believe these truths are for you, too, as you ask the Lord to reframe the way you see your current setting.

1. **Filled.** Joseph, through his trials in various locales, was given the gift of God's infilling. We see recognition of this from the most powerful leader of the land, who noted that even in prison God had filled Joseph: "Pharaoh asked his officials, 'Can we find anyone else like this man so obviously filled with the spirit of God?'" (Genesis 41:38).
2. **Forward-thinking.** As Joseph lived in the land of Egypt for many years, his past began to fade. We see this in the name of his firstborn son: "Joseph named his older son Manasseh, for he said, 'God has made me forget all my troubles and everyone in my father's family'" (Genesis 41:51).
3. **Fruitful.** In the naming of his other son, we see Joseph understanding that even in exile he could be fruitful: "Joseph named his second son Ephraim, for he said, 'God has made me fruitful in this land of my grief'" (Genesis 41:52).
4. **Forgiving.** When Joseph finally revealed himself to his brothers, he offered them forgiveness. Instead of pushing them away, he beckoned them closer: "'I am Joseph!' he said to his brothers. 'Is my father still alive?' But his brothers were speechless! They were stunned to realize that Joseph was standing there in front of them. 'Please, come closer,' he said to them" (Genesis 45:3-4).

5. **Fearless.** In Joseph's enslavement, entrapment, and then imprisonment, he remained connected to God and his purposes even though the situations must've been frightening. At some point he realized that all this heartache happened for a higher purpose: "I am Joseph, your brother, whom you sold into slavery in Egypt. But don't be upset, and don't be angry with yourselves for selling me to this place. It was God who sent me here ahead of you to preserve your lives" (Genesis 45:4-5).

6. **Faithful.** When Jacob blessed Joseph at the end of Jacob's life, he elaborated on Joseph's faithfulness throughout his life: "Archers attacked him savagely; / they shot at him and harassed him. / But his bow remained taut, / and his arms were strengthened / by the hands of the Mighty One of Jacob, / by the Shepherd, the Rock of Israel" (Genesis 49:23-24).

7. **God-fearing.** Although Joseph could have enacted revenge when he encountered the brothers who had sold him into slavery, he relented and feared God far more than he feared them. He understood that God was the judge: "Joseph replied, 'Don't be afraid of me. Am I God, that I can punish you?'" (Genesis 50:19).

8. **Friendly.** This is perhaps the hardest way to be in difficult settings. When we are harmed by others, our settings are stripped from us, or we are forced into exile or pain, will we be so ready to restory our hearts (through the power of the Spirit within) that we can be friendly to those who have harmed us? Joseph did, and his kindness is invitational: "He reassured them by speaking kindly to them" (Genesis 50:21).[7]

Restorying a setting is the kind of wide-sweeping healing God loves to do in our lives. Like Joseph, we are called to rely on God throughout any ordeal we face and then ask the Lord to give us a new perspective in a new place. Our settings morph throughout our lives. However God restories our settings, the one constant is the reassurance of his withness in those places. He will never leave us. He will walk beside us. He will hold us. We cannot escape his presence: "'Can anyone hide from me in a secret place? / Am I not everywhere in all the heavens and earth?' / says the LORD" (Jeremiah 23:24).

And even when we feel forsaken in a setting, or we feel unseen and untended, we do have the new heaven and the new earth to reorient our expectations. God created us for a place—a perfect setting where all our tears will be wiped away. There will be no mourning or death or disease or heartache (Revelation 21:4). There will no longer be unsafe settings to trigger us and keep us down. Jesus reassures us, "There is more than enough room in my Father's home. If this were not so, would I have told you that I am going to prepare a place for you?" (John 14:2). He will be in that safe setting. He is the safest Savior. We can rest there forever.

I often remind myself of this kind of eschatological mindset, repeating these helpful words to myself: "Our present troubles are small and won't last very long. Yet they produce for us a glory that vastly outweighs them and will last forever! So we don't look at the troubles we can see now; rather, we fix our gaze on things that cannot be seen. For the things we see now will soon be gone, but the things we cannot see will last forever" (2 Corinthians 4:17-18).

I can tend to focus on unsafe settings, miring myself in them. So remembering that unsafe places won't last forever is my act of restorying the narrative. Our pain matters. God is using the difficult places we have found ourselves in to better us, equip us for the next trial, and give us uncountable, unseen rewards.

I don't know if I will ever return to the little white house again. Perhaps once was enough for me. But I do know this: I am not the same girl who lived there. I am healed (and healing), freed, and stronger. That's my prayer for you, too.

Questions for Discussion

1. What is the most peaceful setting you've experienced? Why?
2. In what ways have the settings of your life been safe? Unsafe?
3. Why do you think Joseph continued to have a longing for home, even after all the terrible things that happened to him?
4. If you could change one of the settings of your story, what would it be, and why?
5. Has God redeemed any of your settings? If so, how? Which settings do you still fear?

[illegible] when we push th[illegible] [illegible] we don't grow, we certa[illegible] [illegible] Transcendence [illegible] [illegible] to let others [illegible] make meaning [illegible] others, and the wisdom [illegible]

[illegible]

In short, you may try to [illegible] lots of rain, then rumors, [illegible] and [illegible] you [illegible] it, letting out your story [illegible] past, or gives you [illegible] then move on.

The remaining three are different story structures [illegible] give [illegible] your story upon [illegible] the inverted [illegible] of [illegible] your life. Just [illegible] twenty-year [illegible] relationships that shaped [illegible] experiences. [illegible] can be anything you want—when you [illegible] when you got married [illegible] children, or that [illegible] you accomplished last week. There will [illegible] pivot point to your story [illegible] clear before and after. [illegible] Jesus [illegible] lives, and I've been living [illegible] working [illegible] the results of [illegible] and wild [illegible] experience [illegible] story [illegible] become more [illegible] feeling you [illegible] you [illegible] case, [illegible] a circle on a big piece of paper [illegible] we shared in the d[illegible] your birth [illegible] is the story [illegible] beginning. Detail wh[illegible] you [illegible] way, when you [illegible] something differe[illegible] what kind of difficult [illegible] you faced. Did you have a mom[illegible] of profound change? And what does your life look like now that you've learned so much and you're helping others with their lifestorying?

The chiastic structure may take a little more thought. What wa[illegible]

THREE

Discover the Characters in Your Story

"People come, people go—they'll drift in and out of your life, almost like characters in a favorite book. When you finally close the cover, the characters have told their story and you start up again with another book, complete with new characters and adventures. Then you find yourself focusing on the new ones, not the ones from the past."

NICHOLAS SPARKS, *THE RESCUE*

Peter

Fishing companions made up my life. And my world was small then. When I put net to sea that day, James and John, Zebedee's sons, worked beside me. But the day's fishing had been a fruitless task; our bellies roared loudly as we washed victoryless nets. That's when a man asked a simple favor. A crowd pressed in, and he stepped into my boat as if it were the most natural thing in the world for him to do. An odd assumption by a stranger, but his eyes held something in them that wooed me, rumbled my heart. "Can you push us out into the water?" the stranger asked.

I obeyed, though I am not a man prone to submitting to anyone.

The man spoke of love and weakness and trials and birds. When he finished, he said, "Now go out where it is deeper, and let down your nets to catch some fish."

I called him Master even then. I told him, "We worked hard all last night and didn't catch a thing. But if you say so, I'll let the nets down again." Instantaneously, fish swarmed our nets, so much so that our boats threatened to sink. I had to shout to men ashore to help us with such a surprising haul. I knew instantly that this moment, this man, would change my life forever. I fell at the man's feet—later I learned that his name was Jesus—and said, "Oh, Lord, please leave me—I'm such a sinful man."

He told me, "Don't be afraid! From now on you'll be fishing for people!"

And in an instant, my life changed. Until then a simple fisherman whose life was peopled with a few friends and family, I became a disciple among twelve, a follower among a throng of crowds. And with this change came the deepest friendships of my life . . . and my own loyalty, denial, and restoration. I began that day as Simon Peter, but I am now simply Peter, a rock of the church of Jesus, a man of many friends.

The relationships in our lives—our friends and families and coworkers and even the strangers we encounter—have a profound effect on how we live our stories. Some friendships end. Sometimes we must put boundaries around ourselves and separate from unsafe people—even family members. And there are moments when we despair about relationships, where we can scarcely think of someone without heart palpitations.

Relationships can be complicated and encouraging, painful and healing. But did you know that relationships can also be restoried?

I'm thinking currently of a friendship God saw fit to restore in the most beautiful way. In fact, I just stopped to text this friend to see how she was doing today. Through her own broken battle with a church scandal and a series of misunderstandings, our friendship fractured. Most of the onus was on me; I had returned from France a broken person, incapable of handling nuance. Having walked through traumatic relational minefields on the mission field, I had little to no capacity to carry the weight of another's pain. I confess that to you on the page. I was no saint in the breakup of this friendship. In fact, it was me who walked away.

I made a boundary with her, and we stopped communicating, though we had been friends for many, many years. I have plenty of regrets, but I also know that God was the Storyteller of this friendship, and he had something good in store for us both.

When we "broke up," I felt peaceful about letting go, though I grieved deeply the loss of her friendship. I later learned that she grieved similarly.

And then one day I realized that my heart had completely softened toward her, and I felt curious. Through an odd series of events that can only be credited to God's sovereignty, we reconnected. I was sitting in the hammock in my backyard when her voice came through my phone. For three hours we cried, caught up, and spoke life and forgiveness and empathy and words of rewelcoming over each other. I am still in awe of what God did. He loves to turn our mourning into dancing, to take what is seemingly dead and give it breath.

Honestly, I never thought my friend and I would be restoried. But God had beautiful plans I could not have anticipated. Throughout that week, this verse reverberated through me: "No eye has seen, no ear has heard, / and no mind has imagined / what God has prepared / for those who love him" (1 Corinthians 2:9). I felt the heartbeat of God's mysterious ways—the One who confounds us with reconciliations unimaginable.

A restoried relationship may be one that moves toward reconciliation, or it could be that the resolution is in our ability to forgive and release the other person from a safe distance. No matter the courses relationships take, we will experience difficult ones wherever we go. Sometimes God calls us to endure them. Other times we must let some friendships go. Still others may shift and return. I wish there were rubrics to give you—some powerful if-then statements that would help you navigate the roadblocks of human interactions—but the truth is, you have the best relational expert living within you: the Holy Spirit. He himself is a relationship—ever bound and united to God the Father and God the Son. The Trinity exists in a continual flourishing friendship, each member blessing the other. Though the Holy Spirit often gets relegated to third place in people's view of the Godhead (unfortunately), he is the One who dwells inside us. He will comfort us when we're hurt by others, and he will guide us when we need wisdom (John 14:15-31; 2 Corinthians 1:3-7). He understands our stories from beginning to end. He discerns nuance. He knows best how to guide you as you take your next step in a difficult relationship. He loves to give us guidance (James 1:5-6).

The School of Relationships

God uses everything each of us experiences relationally to prepare us for the next part of our journey with others. While it's important to lament relational pain, we can also ask God to give us better resilience, wiser insight, and grittier tenacity as we face the next difficulty. All the things we go through are like the miles we run in obscurity before a big race. We win the race in the mundane, overlooked act of practice. The medal we receive at the race's end has already been earned by sweating behind the scenes.

As I look back on my own dysfunctional family of origin, I realize that all that pain has prepared me today to work through the heartache of leaving a church I loved for many years. Dysfunctional systems are the same, no matter where you experience them. I watched the church leadership morph from embracing healthy practices (welcoming questions, staying open, applauding growth) to taking on familiar unhealthy patterns (quashing dissent, self-protecting at any cost, shunning those who had once helped the church grow). As I was praying about the church situation, this idea swelled in my mind: that God was using my past story to help me navigate this new, terrible one. That knowledge didn't make the pain go away, but it did give me hope that I would survive—after all, I've survived far worse in the past. God has been faithful to me in relational pain before. He sought me, wooed me, and pursued me when I sat mired in dysfunction. If he could rescue me from my family of origin, surely he could rescue me from a toxic church situation.

I also see this truth of being prepared for the next thing when I look back on some predatory work relationships. In my first experience, it took me some time to realize I was being harmed because initially everything went well. I did see lapses in the character of my supervisor, but I liked her so much that I overlooked most red flags, though my stomach was constantly upset during my interactions with her. It was only in retrospect that I was able to untangle everything. A few years later, I found myself in a similar situation with an abusive boss who constantly maligned me, judged me without mercy, and thought the worst of me. As in the earlier situation, my stomach yelled at me, and this time I listened. Once I extricated myself from the situation, relief poured over me. And my upset stomach settled.

Part of restorying relationships is allowing God to show us what choices can help us write healthier stories in the future. In the work situations, I had to ask myself why I had pursued these people in the first place, since they shared similar traits. I wondered if my "picker" was broken. Perhaps something inside me needed a person like that in my life, as though I were completing an unfinished story. Or maybe I wrongly felt that I was healed enough to deal with the toxic person better. One reality, though, was that economic factors gave me little choice but to take those jobs. Sometimes it's not that we're broken and we choose broken people. It may just be that life pushes us toward another difficult relationship. Our task is to (hopefully) discern the situation, extricate ourselves, learn from it, and then move forward.

If I fell into a predatory relationship, I used to think, *That's just how I am. I'm not good at choosing safe people.* That negative loop of thinking tended to trap me in a harmful cycle. I am now learning to embrace the deeper aspects of these astute words from Paul: "We have stopped evaluating others from a human point of view. At one time we thought of Christ merely from a human point of view. How differently we know him now! This means that anyone who belongs to Christ has become a new person. The old life is gone; a new life has begun!" (2 Corinthians 5:16-17).

Go ahead and read the first half of that passage again. Paul instructs us to stop evaluating others from our perspective—from our own logical, typical thinking. People used to know Jesus from a limited point of view, but after his resurrection, their perspective had to expand to embrace the whole Jesus. Similarly, as each of us grows in our own sanctification story, we can shed beliefs that no longer serve us. We can choose to think differently about ourselves. We are no longer held hostage by internal nay-saying statements, thank God. And we are not the sum of our negative thoughts about bad relationships. We have been set free to think differently, live changed, and flourish where we are.

Restorying Relationships

Your relationships can be restoried, but you must leave room for the creativity of God—and you must be willing to recognize that the problem may be you so that you can learn what thoughts or behaviors you can address in yourself before you point the finger at others. As King David aptly prayed, "Search me, O God, and know my heart; / test me and know my anxious thoughts. / Point out anything in me that offends you, / and lead me along the path of everlasting life" (Psalm 139:23-24). I have found that God is faithful to answer such an honest prayer. It takes two to tango *and* to tangle. As disciples of Jesus, we must ask the Lord to sift through our hearts and be humble enough to hear what he has to say.*

So how do we restory our relationships? In talking with audiences around the world, I've seen three ways we work through our relational stress.

Them

Sometimes in our reactions to difficult relationships we overemphasize *them*—other people. When it comes to our relational stories, we can, unfortunately, give people far too much power. In those two difficult work situations I mentioned, I allowed the harshness of both supervisors to completely overwhelm me. Their words seeped into my mood. I ruminated about how I could have responded (like many, I am seldom clever in the moment—only in retrospect). In another instance, I allowed a relative to hold such sway over me that I viewed that person as figuratively ten feet tall. Only when I stood up to these bullies did they shrink (and believe me, it took everything inside me and the power of the Holy Spirit to speak the truth in love in those situations).

* An important caveat: If a relationship is abusive or predatory, it is good and right to protect yourself. In the past I often felt like I had to be a doormat for Jesus—because wasn't that what "turn the other cheek" meant? I've since realized that Jesus truly loves me (and you), which means we are worthy of protection.

Consider what the Word of God instructs when it comes to giving people too much power in your life:

- *People can't cause you to faint.* "Think constantly of him enduring all that sinful men could say against him and you will not lose your purpose or your courage" (Hebrews 12:3, PHILLIPS).
- *Pleasing people solely is antithetical to following Jesus.* "Obviously, I'm not trying to win the approval of people, but of God. If pleasing people were my goal, I would not be Christ's servant" (Galatians 1:10).
- *Trusting people solely, rather than fully trusting Jesus, will lead to heartache.* "Because of the miraculous signs Jesus did in Jerusalem at the Passover celebration, many began to trust in him. But Jesus didn't trust them, because he knew all about people. No one needed to tell him about human nature, for he knew what was in each person's heart" (John 2:23-25).
- *Needing human approval undermines your relationship with God. His approval matters most.* "Many people did believe in him. . . . But they wouldn't admit it. . . . For they loved human praise more than the praise of God" (John 12:42-43).
- *Completely relying on others (without recalling the sinfulness of all of us) can lead to feelings of helplessness.* "Don't put your confidence in powerful people; / there is no help for you there" (Psalm 146:3).
- *Preferring our parents' opinions to the nod of Christ reveals where we are in our relationship with Jesus.* "He who loves father or mother more than Me is not worthy of Me. And he who loves son or daughter more than Me is not worthy of Me" (Matthew 10:37, NKJV).

The people in your life

- are responsible for their own choices;
- don't have permission to control you;
- don't get to ruin your day with their bad behavior;
- don't need you to rescue them by complying with their demands;
- can't sever your relationships with others;
- can't jeopardize your relationship with God;
- aren't your providers—God is—even if they hold sway over your livelihood or salary;
- can't steal your joy;
- aren't being harmed by your good, strong, kindhearted boundaries;
- don't get to tie their well-being to your behavior;
- don't have control over how you respond to their threats; and
- don't have the right to force you to do something you're uncomfortable with, no matter how angry they are.

When we give others too much sway and power in our lives, we won't be living the flourishing relational stories God longs to give us. If someone's behavior or speech continually ruins our joy, then we must consider that that person might be an idol in our lives.

Does that word surprise you? For the Israelites, idolatry ultimately meant worshiping something other than God and chasing after ideas and people who undermined their purpose to be a light to the world. Similarly, an idol for us today is something we look to or run to first, someone or something other than God that we hope to please. (You can learn more about idolatry by doing a simple word search for *idol* in your favorite Bible software.) People are not always idols, but it's important for us to discern whether someone may be acting as one in our lives. We can ask questions like these:

- *Do this person's reactions change the tenor of my day?*
- *Do I change my behavior to appease this person?*
- *Do I become someone else so that this person doesn't judge me?*
- *Am I constantly afraid around this person?*
- *What does my body do when I hear this person's voice?*
- *Do they have power over my emotions and mood? If so, why?*

We dismantle people-as-idols when we accept that we cannot change other people. We stop giving them power when we remember that we are only in charge of our reactions to them.

This may be Relationships 101, but sometimes the simplest things are what help us navigate painful journeys. I've found the term *apatheia* to be helpful when I'm reminding myself what I can and can't control: *Apatheia*, "often translated as 'imperturbability' or 'tranquility,' is a state of being free from negative emotions and passions. That doesn't mean that the Stoics believed in suppressing or denying their emotions, but rather, they strived to cultivate a detached and rational perspective that allowed them to avoid being controlled by their emotions."[1]

We all need a little *apatheia* in our lives. My husband, for example, can detach and look at a situation without emotion-tinted glasses. At first this trait frustrated me, but now I see it as wise. As Stoic philosopher Epictetus writes, "It isn't the things themselves that disturb people, but the judgements that they form about them."[2]

We can spend a lot of time trying to analyze another person or let them get under our skin. But this is not fruitful, and it can cause us to amplify another person's voice over God's. I have often told audiences that our task shouldn't be punishing the villains in our lives but enlarging the God who heals us from all wounds. Instead of spending an inordinate amount of time trying to understand, make a case against, judge rightly, and pass a sentence on someone, we should place our worries, cares, and entanglements into the hands of Jesus.

When it came to my father, I struggled with this. Even after his death, he held gigantic power over me, particularly because I could not figure out why he had been predatory, sometimes criminally so. I pored over true crime books and podcasts trying to understand who he was. I wrongly believed that if I could "figure him out," I could close that painful chapter in my life and move on. The problem was that there was always something more to uncover. And his predatory ways still made no sense to me.

When our relational focus becomes locked on *them*, we put ourselves in an impossible position, because none of us has the power to control or know the mind of another human being. But restorying can free us. What happens when we choose to reframe the narrative spiral that traps us and instead acknowledge the tension and complexity of relationships with other human beings?

I did this as I processed my relationship with my father, writing a fictional scene that set me free from this mental entanglement. Here's a portion of a letter my protagonist, Claire, finds that addresses her need to understand her enigmatic father:

You've spent your adult life asking why your father behaved the way he did. Hear me when I say this: It's unknowable. Remember Jeremiah 17:9, "The human heart is the most deceitful of all things, / and desperately wicked. / Who really knows how bad it is?" I used to think that this solely applied to me, that I could not discern my own bent toward sin. Sure, there is truth to that, but as a follower of Christ, I must rest in the fact that the Holy Spirit within me is doing his beautiful work and will show me my waywardness—because he knows me. He discerns me. He gets me. But we are not allowed to understand evil. Because that is the root of the first sin, isn't it? Trying to know both good and evil? I have found that to spend one's life trying to uncover the intricacies of someone else's interior bent is fruitless. And soul killing.

Why did Ralph treat me as if I were no greater than an old shoe? I don't rightly know.

Why did your father kill your sister? Why did he take all those photos? Why did he obsessively sew for you? (Yes, your mom told me.) Why did he treat your mother with disdain? Why did he chase other women? We don't know. And even if you perfectly understood your father's why, it would not satisfy you. Because evil's reasons are based on pure, unadulterated self-centeredness. Evil is about selfishness and pride (also sins from the garden of Eden). It's about ego and maintaining control at any cost—even the cost of others' well-being. You cannot understand it. You cannot know it. If you spend your life trying to uncover it, you'll slip into depression, like I did. Please, dear Claire, hear me: Let it go. Let him be evil without explanation. His actions are not your responsibility. Neither is his heart. That is the realm of God, who is the perfect Judge.

Sadly, sometimes people enjoy hurting others.

My gift to you today is release. I want you to find a stone from our property, one you can easily hold. Write your father's name on it, and then venture northward to one of the D-Day beaches. But be sure you have some privacy, because I want you to holler at that stone. Tell your dad what you think of him. (Last I heard you had not spoken to him since before the trial. That may have changed, but that reality won't change the importance of this task.) Yell it if you have to. Have a good cry. Let him be who he was. Tell yourself you no longer need to figure it all out. Let it go, dear Claire. Then, with everything inside you, hurl that rock into the North Atlantic. Watch the rock sink to the deep.

And by all that is good, let it remain there.

I haven't finished that novel, but it served its purpose because of this scene. Even reading the letter now brings tears to my eyes, not because of eloquence but because of truth. We are not meant to understand evil. We are intended to know good.

I may eventually get back to that book, but in writing it, I received exactly what I needed. I'm free. I no longer need to search for the why. I pray that this encourages you, too, as you realize that the giants in your life who have held so much sway are as small as the Wizard of Oz, pulling levers behind a curtain.

Him

When other people's voices shout louder than our Creator's "still small voice" (1 Kings 19:12, NKJV), it's a sign that we've begun to de-emphasize God. The more we worry about what other people think, the less we bother ourselves with what God thinks.

Consider Jesus' admonishment to the church at Ephesus: "I have this against you, that you have left your first love" (Revelation 2:4, NKJV). In the "love God, love others" mandate, we must remember that loving God comes first and foremost. He is our reason. He deserves our undivided attention. His opinion should sway us, and as we focus on his voice, the world's clamor will die down.

But even when we stray in our stories, God often pursues us—not with demands but with a quiet wooing, a welcoming of our agency. We get to choose him as our first love, and in that choosing, he gives us a choice about our healing. I'm reminded of the powerful exchange my friend Shannon, a young widow, had with the Lord as she was working through her healing journey:

> One of the things God spoke to me about is choosing healing, choosing him. I wrote in my journal that my heart had a door, and a long time ago I slammed it and threw the key as far as I could. I kept that door barricaded for years, not allowing anyone in—even Jesus. It seemed safest that way, to protect myself from more hurt. But God found that key, and he gently placed it in my palm. I heard him saying (not audibly, but you know what I mean), "Shannon, here's the key. It's now in your hand. You can choose. I will not break in. I will not force myself on you. Know that I am here and waiting."[3]

Friend, that's the beauty of our restoried life with God. He gives us the choice. And when we use our keys to open the door to him, we begin to reframe all our painful relationships. Is it scary to open ourselves up to God and then others? Yes. But doing so is part of recognizing and trusting our first love: the God who exists in relationship, who leads us through our relationships, and who heals us from the difficult ones.

Us

When we underestimate God, we can also be guilty of de-emphasizing people. While we shouldn't value others' opinions over the Lord's, we also cannot dismiss how God heals relational wounds. A relational wound requires a relational cure. If you are wounded by people, God asks you to step into a safe relationship to heal.

There is a profound difference between creating a fence around your emotional yard and erecting a fortress that no one can enter.

Barricading our hearts seems to make all the sense in the world—after all, why go back to places where we've been deeply wounded? But when we put up walls, we cut ourselves off from the path to healing. Creating elaborate scaffolding around ourselves may protect us from emotional harm, but it will also push away joy. When we live out of self-protection, the result is isolation, not health. And God's Word tells us, "Whoever isolates himself seeks his own desire; / he breaks out against all sound judgment" (Proverbs 18:1, ESV).

If we want thriving, flourishing lives, we must embrace the people God brings our way, even if we're afraid. These folks may be who God wants to use for our healing. You might think, *Well, they might hurt me too, and then where would that leave me?* I certainly would not counsel you to cavalierly stampede into random relationships, particularly if you've been traumatically hurt. Of course you should give yourself some time to work through your grief. But there will come a time when you'll be presented with a pathway toward healing through another person. Maybe stick a toe into that pool and test it out. Then submerge your ankles to discover whether the water is good and confirm that there are no alligators in it.

Relationships broke me and my family when we were church planters in France, but good relationships brought profound healing in the aftermath. It is a risk. But it is possible.

If it's frightening for you to entrust yourself to another person (and that is a very tender, difficult thing), consider the times in your life when you've had the privilege of bearing another's burden. How would you feel if the person you loved walked away from you, their anxiety becoming the catalyst for rejection? We are called to bear each other's burdens, but if no one is vulnerable enough to welcome another person into their pain, none of us will have the joy of doing so. It is a gift to ask for help. And a gift to be asked.

Restorying Peter

A rough-and-tumble fisherman who spoke his mind and gave into his passions, the apostle Peter would not have the story he is praised for had he not had relationships. His relationship with Jesus deeply shaped who he became, particularly when he was restored even after three vehement denials of the relationship. And his relationships with the other disciples became the foundation of the church that would spread its tendrils throughout the world. These were not always easy friendships—consider when the apostle Paul publicly confronted Peter about his favoritism toward Jews (see Galatians 2:11-21)! But Peter, who sinned boldly and then humbled himself quickly, restoried the way he treated Gentiles because of the iron-sharpening-iron nature (Proverbs 27:17) of his relationships.

The Kingdom of God is not about solo people winning souls—it is about a group of folks sharing the love of Jesus with each other and the world, working alongside each other to bring about healing and restorying each other back to life.

Questions for Discussion

1. How do you think the people in Peter's life (including Jesus) influenced him?
2. When have people been "too big" or their voices too loud in your life? What happened?
3. Have you walked through a trial when, in retrospect, God seemed small? Why do you think that was?
4. What do you need to demonstrate *apatheia* toward right now?
5. Who are the most significant people in your life who have taught you about following Jesus?

[illegible] we don't grow. We certai[illegible] [illegible] what's been done [illegible] [illegible] to let others [illegible] others, and the wisdom [illegible]

Self-editing your story [illegible]

[illegible]

Li[illegible], you may try to [illegible] your past [illegible] lens of [illegible] and surpass you, leaving you [illegible] place, unable to grow beyo[illegible] it. [illegible] your story [illegible] from [illegible] your past and gives you space [illegible] heal—and then move on.

The [illegible] different story structures in [illegible] give [illegible] your story upon. [illegible] simple [illegible] (the inverted [illegible]) [illegible] of [illegible] points in your life. Just to [illegible] [illegible] relationships that shaped [illegible] you want—when you [illegible] when you got married, [illegible] children, or [illegible] last week. There [illegible] pivot point to your story [illegible] before, then after. [illegible] traumatic things [illegible] early life. [illegible] Jesus [illegible] fifteen, and I've been living [illegible] working hard to show the results [illegible] with fear, reverence and fear" [illegible] began, and to be quite honest, I'm still [illegible] healing journey.

Or perhaps you [illegible] In that case, [illegible] I've shared in the [illegible] your birth [illegible] beginning. Detail whe[illegible] you [illegible] something differen[illegible] what kind of difficulties [illegible] you faced. Did you have a mom[illegible] of profound change? And what does your life look like now that you've learned so much and you're helping others with their restorying?

The chiastic structure may take a little more thought. What wa[illegible] the main pivot in your life? It could be a decision to stop drinkin[illegible]

FOUR

Identify Your Inciting Incidents

"The inciting incident is how you get [characters] to do something. . . . It's the doorway through which they can't return, you know. The story takes care of the rest."

BEN PEARSON, QUOTED IN DONALD MILLER, *A MILLION MILES IN A THOUSAND YEARS*

Paul

I considered myself a Jew among Jews, zealous for the things of God. Growing up in the Mediterranean city of Tarsus, a center of culture and learning, I enjoyed talking with others about contemporary literature and the musings of philosophy. But most of all I loved the Torah and the prophets of old. I was the son of a Pharisee, and I trained extensively under the tutelage of Gamaliel, himself a Pharisee of Pharisees. Righteous zeal defined my life: I loved my people, and I felt protective of them, particularly when it came to sects and their strange teachings, which were constantly infiltrating our faith.

When I encountered the Way, I knew that this philosophy—centered around someone named Jesus—would prove to be a destructive heresy in need of quashing. In my zeal, I took it upon myself to cleanse my people of this scourge. I went house to house, rooting out dissent. Who I was, how I was raised, and the man I had become felt deeply empowered to save our God from these miscreants. Perhaps my most zealous act came at the stoning of a man named Stephen, who claimed to see this Jesus standing (standing!) at the right hand of the throne of God as the stones wrecked his life. I wholeheartedly celebrated his righteous punishment, believing myself to be the protector of all things Jewish.

But then.

Oh, then.

As I went along toward Damascus with letters in hand to condemn more people to judgment, a bright light blinded me from heaven, and a strong voice poured over me, asking me why I was persecuting him. It was the voice of the One I persecuted with such abandon. This Jesus called me away from my crusade into another area entirely—to win the pagan nations to himself.

I saw myself clearly now: I had been a blasphemer, a murderer, and in all that, self-righteous to my bones. But God, in his infinite wisdom, chose me, the least of all, to become his mouthpiece to a dying world.

I often wondered how my background could be helpful to the God of the universe, who was himself everything all at once—but Jesus redeemed all my working knowledge of the Law and the Prophets to shape theologies and treatises that are helping form the backbone of the very church of God. Although I count my expertise as rubbish, my past story has helped me as God has redeemed my present story. All those abilities, of course, I count as loss, but at each new story point in my life, I've had the joy and privilege of using my trinkets of understanding for the Kingdom of God.

For that I am grateful.

Think of your favorite story. What is the moment, the action, that propels the plot forward? What moves the characters to make decisions and move toward changes that will set the direction of their whole story?

That is the inciting incident.

An inciting incident hints at the main conflict of a story, and it's usually life interrupting. Nothing will ever be the same after an inciting incident. In storytelling terms, it's what makes the reader want to keep reading. It's an invitational interruption—and often it involves pain or bewilderment.

The apostle Paul had two lives: the life before Christ and the life after his inciting incident on the road to Damascus, where he was blinded and confronted by God. God used the Kingdom of God to restory Paul's entire future—and it began with a holy intervention. He desires the same for you, friend. He can take the whole of your story, make you whole, and then give you the ability to bring wholeness to a shattered world.

Spotting Inciting Incidents

How can you spot the inciting incidents in your life? One way is to consider the turning points you've experienced along the way—when you saw your life moving one way and then it radically shifted direction, like taking a U-turn. Another way is to consider what events or situations have shaped who you are today. While inciting incidents can often be traumatic events, they can be positive situations as well. Infertility ends with a pregnancy. A job offer comes after months of unemployment. That onetime enemy has now become a friend.

When I look at my own story, I can map out some major plot points connected to inciting incidents. I've shared many of my initial inciting incidents in earlier chapters, but here are some others from my life up to this point:

- *College years.* I was so desperate to heal and so needy for attention that I became an oversharer, but thankfully the Lord surrounded me with people who loved to pray and who dared to believe that God would heal this traumatized girl. So much healing happened during these years that I took a head-in-the-sand approach to the next ten years, believing I had been completely restored to health. Ah, naïveté!
- *Twenty-three years old.* I married Patrick, and we began our lives together. This was my first venture away from my family of origin, and I began truly seeing what I had grown up with. But, true to form, I pushed down most of my pain. We were also in a few churches that encouraged outward happiness, so I kept up a good-girl Christian façade. After all, I had been healed. My husband's love for me began salving my father wounds, though his own parents' abusive and dismissive actions toward us deeply wounded me.
- *Child-birthing and child-rearing years.* Back home in Washington state, we had three kids in six years. After all my family brokenness, all I had wanted once I got married was to have a family. Our first pregnancy, sadly, was ectopic, but I was thankful to have Sophie, Aidan, and Julia afterward. Terribly tired and unmoored, I did my best to live up to my church's Christian-mother ideal, though I often felt ill-equipped given my background. And when my eldest turned five, the age I was when so much profound abuse had happened to me, I quickly realized that I had a lot more healing to walk through, so I pursued it as well as I could.
- *Thirty-one years old.* We made our first cross-cultural move from Seattle to Palestine, East Texas, for Patrick's job. Our

marriage had experienced some difficult bumps, but here in the piney woods we began to heal. During this time, Patrick felt God calling him to ministry, and I started writing in earnest, garnering my first published article.

- *Thirty-three years old.* We moved from Palestine to the Dallas area so Patrick could attend Dallas Theological Seminary. These four years I spent beginning my writing career and continuing to raise the kids.
- *Thirty-seven years old.* This was our last cross-cultural move, from Texas to outside Nice, France. We were church planters for nearly three years. After the experiences and traumas we walked through there, we were diagnosed with PTSD. We'd lost our home back in the States to a con man we'd met through a prayer team at church; our team had exploded several times; we'd uncovered wolves in sheep's clothing among our leadership; our kids had struggled deeply with school and peers. And on top of it all were culture shock, overwork, and depression.
- *The rebuilding years.* In my late thirties and early to late forties, after we'd returned from the mission field, we worked through the trauma we'd all experienced in France. The kids had varying responses to their time there that we had to work through, some very troubling and scary. We continued to serve in our beloved church as life group leaders. I pioneered two conferences and a Lifeway study recording and continued writing about three books a year.
- *2019.* This was the year I stepped into a more public role as an advocate for sexual abuse survivors, wrote *We Too: How the Church Can Respond Redemptively to the Sexual Abuse Crisis*, and went onstage at the Southern Baptist Convention annual

meeting to pray for those who had been abused. The advocacy leveled me, and I had to take a sabbatical to recover.

- *The present day.* We are walking through one of the most painful inciting incidents I've experienced, and it's one that I did not anticipate. Though I have written about celebrity pastors and churches and spiritual abuse, my own experience of those things in the past has been relatively scant. But we have now had to leave the church we loved and raised our kids in—a church we called home for twenty-three years. This has whiplashed me back to 2019, when I advocated for victims, because it feels eerily similar (and hauntingly futile). I need rest. We are grateful we've found a new church, but walking through this valley has been devastating.

As you identify your own inciting incidents, you can write them down or record them in your phone. The point of this kind of exercise is to uncover similarities, patterns, and redemptive threads. As you do, you can be completely honest. Ask questions like *Why did this happen?* or *Jesus, why didn't you rescue me from this?*

There are many practical ways to approach plotting your inciting incidents. They don't have to be about your life in general: When I train writers, I ask each of them to create a story arc of their writing journey. (It's fascinating to see how God has moved in writers' lives to bring them to where they are today in their book-writing endeavors.) Some have traced their spiritual journeys in the same way. Still others have traced their inciting incidents around relationships. I followed a timeline approach, sharing plot points in chronological order. Another way to work through this is to shift your orientation from that of a close narrator (first person) to an omniscient narrator (as if God were telling your story). How would your story differ if God were recounting it? Or how would another person narrate your journey in third person? In thinking through these different ways to see our plot points, we gain a deeper understanding of how things fit together.

In looking at our stories, our goal is to see connections, to find ways the Lord is "caus[ing] everything to work together for the good of those who love God and are called according to his purpose for them" (Romans 8:28). In Psalm 139, we see King David's own timeline of events, but with an eye toward God's hand in his life: "O Lord, you have examined my heart / and know everything about me. / You know when I sit down or stand up. / You know my thoughts even when I'm far away. / You see me when I travel / and when I rest at home. / You know everything I do" (Psalm 139:1-3). I encourage you to read through this psalm several times as you contemplate examining your own story. There is powerful reassurance in knowing that God sees us, knows us intimately, and carries us through our stories. When I'm anxious about the future, I have found solace in these words: "You saw me before I was born. / Every day of my life was recorded in your book. / Every moment was laid out / before a single day had passed" (Psalm 139:16). I may be able to record what has happened in the past, I can ask God to give me insight into what he is doing in my life in the present, and I can rejoice that he knows all my days—even my final ones.

As I look back on my life, I'm reminded of its brevity. I echo the sentiments of the psalmist when he pens, "Teach us to realize the brevity of life, / so that we may grow in wisdom. / O Lord, come back to us! / How long will you delay? / Take pity on your servants! / Satisfy us each morning with your unfailing love, / so we may sing for joy to the end of our lives" (Psalm 90:12-14). It's my sincere desire to sing for joy as I approach eternity; it is my hope for you, too. Life is fleeting. It's a vapor, according to the author of Ecclesiastes (see Ecclesiastes 1:2)[1]—a hiccup in time. We must do what we can in the time we've been given. Paul reminds us, "Be careful how you live. Don't live like fools, but like those who are wise. Make the most of every opportunity in these evil days" (Ephesians 5:15-16).

A Time to Notice

For everything there is a season,
a time for every activity under heaven.
ECCLESIASTIES 3:1

Our stories are multifaceted. There is never a moment when every duck is lined up in its proverbial row. Life is too complicated for that—and too beautiful. We exist in seasons, and our joyfulness rides upon our ability to accept whatever season we're in.

As I was writing this book, a friend of mine lost her husband. His death was sudden and shocking. We spend our lives trying to avoid demise (rightly so), but it's the specter that keeps haunting, continually reminding us of life's swift brevity. We may know the "once upon a time" of our stories, but few of us discern "the end."

There's something sobering yet clarifying about death. The writer of Ecclesiastes advises, "Better to spend your time at funerals than at parties. / After all, everyone dies— / so the living should take this to heart. / Sorrow is better than laughter, / for sadness has a refining influence on us" (Ecclesiastes 7:2-3). Being aware of the end of your story can serve as a reminder to stop and see.

I have found Ecclesiastes, particularly Ecclesiastes 3:1-15, a helpful way to frame my perspective in the good and hard incidents of life. Taking a step back to consider what "time" we are in—and what that time is for—is a crucial part of allowing God to restory us. The principle beneath Ecclesiastes is paying attention, taking notice, observing.

Be where you are right now. See what is happening. Process it with the Lord, a friend, your journal. Be in it. When we are still, we are better able to discern what inciting incident God has for us. But if we move quickly through, we may miss what he is trying to teach us.

The inciting incidents in your story are entry points to new seasons—some hard, some beautiful. Noticing the ebb and flow of the painful and the good, and God's faithfulness amid it all, will help you weather the inciting incidents to come.

Notice Your Losses

A time to be born and a time to die.
A time to plant and a time to harvest.
ECCLESIASTES 3:2

If you're like me, you may be tired of all the refining that comes with inciting incidents. Grief is its own cloud, yet part of the restory process is noticing how loss begets growth. Jesus reminds us of this paradox, that death precedes life: "I tell you the truth, unless a kernel of wheat is planted in the soil and dies, it remains alone. But its death will produce many new kernels—a plentiful harvest of new lives" (John 12:24). There is a time to start things, to sow a seed into the soil in view of a potential harvest.

To harvest, we must first dream, then plant, then allow our little seed to die so that it can produce a harvest eventually. I'm currently walking through a season of grief over church hurt, and I'm desperately trying to think about what it could look like to start something new. As my husband and I recently walked at our park, our chocolate Lab happily ignorant of the weight of my soul, I asked Patrick, "How can I get out of this depression? How can I be healthy again?"

"You need to pay attention to the little things," he told me. "And see the new place where we are as an adventure."

He's right. In the old song "Things We Leave Behind," Michael Card sings of the unimaginable freedom we uncover only after we leave other things behind.[2] The song became my anthem when we moved from the Washington peninsulas area to a northern Seattle suburb. We left a good church, friends, and a happy life. But we also had the opportunity to meet a whole new group of friends and a beautiful congregation, and that little kernel of longing to be a writer began to flourish in that place. C. S. Lewis reminds us in *The Last Battle* that we are to move "further up and further in."[3] We are constantly on an adventure of moving forward. We cannot change the past, but we can live in this moment with intention, and because of what Jesus has laid hold of for us, we can joyfully anticipate the future. Paul writes, "No, dear brothers and sisters, I have not achieved it, but I focus on this one thing: Forgetting the past and looking forward to what lies ahead, I press on to reach the end of the race and receive the heavenly prize for which God, through Christ Jesus, is calling us" (Philippians 3:13-14). Even in death, we think of planting, then the harvest.

Notice Your Emotions

A time to kill and a time to heal.
A time to tear down and a time to build up.
A time to cry and a time to laugh.
A time to grieve and a time to dance.
ECCLESIASTES 3:3-4

Our lives are full of ending one thing and beginning another, moving from tears to laughter (sometimes in the same hour). Knowing these sacred rhythms helps us endure each incident as it arises, giving us the kind of perspective we need when it's time to tear something down and leave it behind. In short, it's important to pay attention to our emotions. In his excellent book *Necessary Endings*, Dr. Henry Cloud shares an important truth: "In the language of Ecclesiastes, are there situations in business or in life where you are trying to birth things that should be dying? Trying to heal something that should be killed off? Laughing at something that you should be weeping about? Embracing something (or someone) you should shun? Searching for an answer for something when it is time to give up? Continuing to try to love something or someone when it is time to talk about what you hate?"[4]

In working through your plot points, perhaps you're seeing that it's time to end that relationship or move on from that job situation. Pay close attention to how you feel in each situation. Perhaps you're realizing as you read this that one of your inciting incidents, in the form of a relationship, needs some holy editing. While emotions can be fickle, they can also be signposts of things that are not quite right.

Notice God's Plan

A time to scatter stones and a time to gather stones.
A time to embrace and a time to turn away.
A time to search and a time to quit searching.
A time to keep and a time to throw away.

ECCLESIASTES 3:5-6

When I was in college, I dated a guy who was my first love (yeah, I was a late bloomer). When he broke up with me, my world crashed. I had hung all my hopes on our future, and I couldn't understand why God would do such a terrible thing. I drove hours to the Pacific coast while the rain drenched my car, and then I pulled out my Bible and did that thing you're not supposed to do—open it willy-nilly and pray that the Lord will speak to you.

The verse about scattering and gathering stones appeared before me. I got out of my warm car while sideways rain pelted me, intermingling with my tears. I gathered as many stones as I could while my shoes got soaked. Each represented a hope I had or a heartache I was walking through. With all the might I could muster, I hurled stone after stone into the ocean, weeping as I did.

And now, in retrospect, I'm grateful God scattered those relational hopes, let them sink deep into the waves. What I thought was unkindness on his part was God's never-ending love, preventing me from making a painful mistake. I had once embraced that boyfriend, and now he had turned away. I had once sought solace as I'd constantly searched for his love (he was fickle in his affections), but now in not searching I could heal. As he had discarded me, I learned (eventually) to let him go.

As you look back on your life, what perspective on God's plan do you have now that you didn't have before? In the moment of the heartache, you couldn't possibly see any good coming from it, but now you see God's powerful protection or sustenance. Perhaps he grew you through the pain. What one inciting incident meant for evil, God meant for your good (see Genesis 50:20). It just took time to get there.

All this is to say: Be patient. Trust that God sees every nuance of your current pain. It may feel bleak right now, but the story hasn't ended.

Notice Your Season

A time to tear and a time to mend.
A time to be quiet and a time to speak.
A time to love and a time to hate.
A time for war and a time for peace.

ECCLESIASTES 3:7-8

We have seasons of rending and mending, silence and proclamation, contending and peacemaking. Part of living a restoried life is simply recognizing what kind of inciting incident you're experiencing.

In his excellent book *Spiritual Rhythm: Being with Jesus Every Season of Your Soul,* Mark Buchanan elaborates, "Then God gave me insight: this was winter. It would end, in time, but not by my own doing. My responsibility was simply to know the season, and match my actions and inactions to it. It was to learn the slow hard discipline of waiting. It was my season to believe *in spite of*—to believe in the absence of evidence or emotion, when there's nothing, no bud, no color, no light, no birdsong, to validate belief. It was my time to walk without sight."[5]

As you look back on your story, it may be helpful to discern your springs, summers, autumns, and winters. And then ask yourself: *What season am I in today? And how should I adjust my expectations accordingly?*

As the poetry of Ecclesiastes 3 ends, the author turns toward prose:

> What do people really get for all their hard work? I have seen the burden God has placed on us all. Yet God has made everything beautiful for its own time. He has planted eternity in the human heart, but even so, people cannot see the whole scope of God's work from beginning to end. So I concluded there is nothing better than to be happy and enjoy ourselves as long as we can. And people should eat and drink and enjoy the fruits of their labor, for these are gifts from God.
>
> And I know that whatever God does is final. Nothing can be added to it or taken from it. God's purpose is that people should fear him. What is happening now has happened before, and what will happen in the future has happened before, because God makes the same things happen over and over again.
>
> ECCLESIASTES 3:9-15

There is much wisdom we can glean from these declarative sentences, and they have direct implications as we plot our turning points:

- We may not see the positives of a situation today, but God is able to eke out beauty from it.

- When we maintain an eternal perspective (which God grants us), our daily plot points take on significance.
- During a hard season, it's good to seek enjoyment, to do as my husband reminded me: Find joy in small places.
- It is permissible (and commendable) to delight in the fruits of your labor. (As a person who is exceedingly thrifty, this is hard for me to do.)
- God's plans will prevail. His purposes last. This takes pressure off us to "make life work." We can rest in his sovereignty, even when our plot points seem random or devastating or confusing.

Restorying Paul

Ecclesiastes reminds us that there is nothing new under the sun (Ecclesiastes 1:9). That's why reading and studying is so important—because we can learn from those who have faced similar things to what we are facing. I fear that we have so distanced ourselves from the Bible that we forget that the people populating its pages are not characters but were real, living human beings. Learning about the inciting incidents of their lives—and how their lives changed in the aftermath—can help us understand our own.

The apostle Paul certainly had a lightning bolt of an inciting incident on the road to Damascus. Before that fulcrum, Paul was a persecutor of the church; afterward, he became a pillar of it. He moved from ridiculing the Way to worshiping the Son, who had inaugurated the Way. He who had once persecuted the followers of Jesus would endure persecution in the name of Jesus.

While you may not have such a blatant turning-point moment, chances are that Jesus intersected your life at one point, changing the trajectory of it. He is the best possible inciting incident! As you look at the turning points in your story, may you see his hand throughout them all—redeeming what's been lost, restorying what has been harmful, refreshing that which has devastated you. Our lives are an ever-expanding adventure, and our Lord is an ever-present Story Recrafter.

Questions for Discussion

1. As you look back on your life, what would you consider to be the most significant (positive or negative) inciting incidents you've experienced?
2. Which perspective from Ecclesiastes 3 helps you restory your inciting incidents right now?
3. What does Paul's encounter on the road to Damascus teach you about turning points? Does an inciting incident always have to be spectacular (like Paul's)? What small U-turn have you experienced lately?
4. Consider a time you've had a perspective change about an inciting incident. How did you see the incident at first? How do you understand it now?
5. How can reframing your life as an adventure help you work through the next transition points in your story?

[illegible]

of profound change? And what does your life look like now that you've learned so much and you're helping others with their restorying?

The chiastic structure may take a little more thought. What wa

FIVE

Endure the Muddled Middle

When you are in the middle of a story it isn't a story at all, but only a confusion; a dark roaring, a blindness, a wreckage of shattered glass and splintered wood; like a house in a whirlwind, or else a boat crushed by the icebergs or swept over the rapids, and all aboard powerless to stop it. It's only afterwards that it becomes anything like a story at all. When you are telling it, to yourself or to someone else.

MARGARET ATWOOD, *ALIAS GRACE*

The Woman with the Issue of Blood

I scarce can remember a life of vitality, of thriving, of warm skin. The moment the bleeding began, I expected it to stop—as was the way of young women. I had thrilled that I could now bear a child, but that joy became short-lived when the bleeding continued. And continued. And never stopped. With each miracle cure, my anticipation rose, only to drop me into despair when I kept hemorrhaging. Physician after physician. Holy man after holy man. Prayer after prayer. Nothing worked.

Beyond that, I was deemed unclean by my community, unable to participate in the religious life of my people. This brought its own isolation, and it cemented my feelings of unworthiness. How would I ever marry? (I wouldn't.) How would I ever carry children? (I wouldn't.) How would I ever live to see old age? (I don't think I will.)

Grief haunts me at every turn. So much loss. The pain of empty relationships, the sting of rejection, the mourning of what I want but will never come to pass—these heartaches are the blood coursing through my veins, only to spill onto the ground and be absorbed by the dust. So many times I rise in that avian way, wings flapping toward hope, only to flutter, fluster, then plummet to the earth. I am learning that hope is a dangerous thing.

But I have heard there is One who heals the likes of me. One who is kind yet powerful. Strong yet gentle. Who seems to understand the plight of outcasts.

It takes everything inside me to dare to approach this Physician of sorts. I am so weak and—to be honest—terrified. I can barely walk. But I see him up ahead, and I must at least force myself to take another step.

I fall in the dusty street, place my head to the ground, and pray for the strength to rise again, but I cannot. So I crawl in the shaded place beneath the crowd, avoiding feet, hoping I'm heading in the right direction. Isn't this how I have had to live my life as an unclean woman longing for healing? Always hoping I'm going the right way—only to be thwarted again?

I believe I finally reach the man, but I am too weak to stand and make my request. He is so important that, perhaps, he wouldn't even hold my gaze. So I think, Maybe it's enough to simply touch the hem of his cloak. *I reach out toward the fringe, saying one last desperate prayer, and then . . .*

The warmth starts at the middle of my body, spreading outward toward my limbs. The stream of blood ceases. And I can stand and make my escape. I am full of wonder.

"Who touched me?"

The voice is his, but I am frightened.

His companions rightly chide the man. So many people have touched him on this crowded street! Surely he is not speaking of me.

But then I know. He speaks of the power that left him but touched me. I, who am finally able to stand with the confidence that comes without fear of fainting, bow at his beautiful feet. Trembling, I recount my story of grief and pain to this beautiful man. The words spill from me like an overflowing river. So many levels to my story. I want to rush through, but I sense his desire for me to slow down and say it all. In that moment, I am being set free from the shackles of who I thought I was. I was an invalid, but now he is validating me. I was inflamed, but now I am ignited with power. I study his face. I must remember his eyes.

He lifts me from my position in the dust, and I feel more strength enter my once-weakened body.

"Daughter," he calls me. "Your faith has made you well. Go in peace. Your suffering is over."

As a novelist, I am quite aware of the muddled middle. It's the point in the story when the characters seem to be in suspended animation. They're awaiting action, but the author has no real plans for them. Instead, the cast talks in circles, repeats the same mistakes, and seems to do things but never arrive or grow.

Have you ever felt that way? Have you experienced a stagnation that deeply wounds you? Are there prayers unanswered that keep you up at night? Do you feel like there's no movement in your life and that you're simply going through the motions, deeply discouraged and unable to pull yourself from the mire?

Welcome to the muddled middle.

The middle of a mess is a place none of us prefer. In some ways it's better to be in the thick of things because we can at least *do* something. Or even better, to have the muddled middle in retrospect because it's always nicer to have a mess in life's rearview mirror.

But the muddled middle is part of every story. And no matter how bewildering we find it, God has a plan for restorying even this.

Waiting Is Normal

We see the Word of God peopled with folks who don't get what they want immediately. Noah built an ark with ridicule as his backdrop. Abraham had to sojourn and live in tents. Sarah waited decades before she birthed Isaac. Moses lived exiled for forty years before he became Israel's emancipator. Then the nation of Israel wandered in the wilderness before setting foot in the Promised Land. Many of Israel's kings faced war as a chronic obstacle to their complete conquests. The nation of Israel was divided and then lived in exile before they returned, limping, back to the Promised Land as a remnant of what they were before. And in Hebrews 11, we read about many patriarchs and matriarchs who were godly but didn't receive what they were hoping for:

> All these people died still believing what God had promised them. They did not receive what was promised, but they saw it all from a distance and welcomed it. They agreed that they were foreigners and nomads here on earth. Obviously people who say such things are looking forward to a country they can call their own. If they had longed for the country they came from, they could have gone back. But they were looking for a better place, a heavenly homeland. That is why God is not ashamed to be called their God, for he has prepared a city for them.
>
> HEBREWS 11:13-16

Lest we wrongly believe that waiting only happened in the Old Testament, when people awaited the Messiah, we see the disciples in the middle of a waiting game in the first chapter of Acts:

> When the apostles were with Jesus, they kept asking him, "Lord, has the time come for you to free Israel and restore our kingdom?"

He replied, "The Father alone has the authority to set those dates and times, and they are not for you to know."
ACTS 1:6-7

Even now, in the muddled middle of history, we have to wait for God's beautiful denouement.

Friend, waiting is normal.

I wish this weren't true, to be honest. I don't like the idea of waiting, seemingly forever, for a promise to come true. But this is what the Word of God reminds us: Sometimes in our restory journeys, God calls us, along with everyone else, to wait on him. I might secretly hope I will be the exception to the rule, but I am not. We all must yearn and long for the denouement while we wait in the muddled middle.

But the Scriptures have much to say about the discipline of waiting:

- *We are to be brave as we wait.* "Wait patiently for the Lord. / Be brave and courageous. / Yes, wait patiently for the Lord" (Psalm 27:14).
- *Our waiting means we trust that God will act on our behalf.* "Be still in the presence of the Lord, / and wait patiently for him to act. / Don't worry about evil people who prosper / or fret about their wicked schemes" (Psalm 37:7).
- *Waiting involves knowing and believing the trustworthy Word of God.* "I am counting on the Lord; / yes, I am counting on him. / I have put my hope in his word. / I long for the Lord / more than sentries long for the dawn, / yes, more than sentries long for the dawn" (Psalm 130:5-6).
- *Waiting involves a joyful expectation of the surprises of God.* "Since the world began, / no ear has heard / and no eye has seen a God like you, / who works for those who wait for him!" (Isaiah 64:4).

That's all good and right, of course, but you may be saying, *Hey, I'm stuck right now in my own issues, dealing with current stagnation.* I agree with you. I am there with you. I have that holy ache for breakthrough—in fact, there's a worship song, appropriately entitled "Breakthrough," that I keep crying through when I think of my current situation. That longing is real, and it is difficult. The next question becomes *Now what?*

Lessons in the Middle

The muddled middle of an unfinished story gives me time to reflect, particularly if I've been in a similar place before. In my current middle, I've noticed how prone I am to panic, particularly about health issues. But I've been able to look back on my days of excessive stress over the past decade or so and realize that most of that panic came from feeling out of control when it comes to my health. Health, after all, is something I have a semblance of control over but not entire control. Lifestyle and medical interventions can only go so far when a spot is found, when the blood pressure is high, or when I am confronted by aging. In the muddle of the middle, I've been able to realize that I will continue to panic and give in to dramatics if I don't face this issue.

When my husband was in seminary, he preached a sermon based on Proverbs 26:11-12: "As a dog returns to its vomit, / so a fool repeats his foolishness. / There is more hope for fools / than for people who think they are wise." It seemed like such a simple, short passage, but as he unpacked it, we both learned a lot. Too often I think I am wise, able to discern the way through a painful situation. I believe I can use logic to fix it. But often I don't take into account the complexity of my own patterns, my distorted thinking, and the confusing maze of life. I can't possibly know all the mysteries. And if I continue to rely solely on my instincts, I'll keep returning to the same mistakes I've made before.

To be restoried is to identify those repeated pitfalls and then seek help to do better. We typically don't grow in isolation, but it can be helpful to reflect on your own to find emerging patterns. I do this by reading my old journals or looking at the notes in my Bible.

Simply identifying an issue is not enough to overcome it, however. After uncovering my ongoing struggle with aging and body image, I realized I needed help from others in this area. I spent time getting coaching from an expert. I listened to podcasts. I read a few books. I asked several friends to pray with me. I am not perfectly through this area of struggle, but it has been amazing to see how God brings help in the form of others who also struggle.

If you're willing to learn the lessons of the middle, you'll uncover three important perspective shifts: (1) an encouragement toward growth, (2) an awareness of where you've misled yourself, and (3) a transformed perspective on the obstacles in your way.

You Can Discern Your Pathway to Growth

My husband, Patrick, teaches often about the fact that Christianity is not passive but active. Even in the unclear middles of our stories, we can't just hope for growth—we must pursue it. We don't heal by waiting around, expecting it will happen by osmosis. Growth is an active endeavor, a craving.

We see this call to growth, regardless of our circumstances, throughout Scripture. Jesus said in the Sermon on the Mount that "God blesses those who hunger and thirst for justice, / for they will be satisfied" (Matthew 5:6). When we are new Christians, we are called to crave growth: "Like newborn babies, you must crave pure spiritual milk so that you will grow into a full experience of salvation. Cry out for this nourishment, now that you have had a taste of the Lord's kindness" (1 Peter 2:2-3). And we are commanded to continue growing as we walk further in our discipleship journeys: "You must grow in the grace and knowledge of our Lord and Savior Jesus Christ" (2 Peter 3:18).

Growth doesn't happen lackadaisically. But when you're in a

muddled season, your *try* muscle may be tired. Or maybe life has battered you and you don't feel like you have the strength to move, much less grow. That is normal.

The beautiful paradox of your restorying journey is this secret: You've already been given the Spirit, who will empower you toward growth. Consider the woman with the issue of blood. She pursued Jesus, yes, but she merely touched the fringe of his garment. This means she was most likely crawling toward him in the dust. In that tiny moment between her fingers touching his cloak (her feeble pursuit) and complete healing, the Spirit did his miraculous work. Our last bits of effort are met with the power of God.

In the muddled middle, we find what we are made of. Everything is stripped away, and our faith muscles weaken. Thankfully, the Lord doesn't require heroics from us. We can simply pray, *I want to learn from this muddled time. Help me want to. Give me the gumption to keep going. I don't want to keep circling around this area of needed growth—I want to grow through the pain. Can you teach me how?*

When I'm in the muddled middle and I feel the weight of stagnation, I try to remind myself of life's brevity. It's a snapshot, a blink, a flash of lightning. Our afflictions won't last forever, although it feels like we're stuck in the story's belly. We can memorize these encouraging and pointed words from Paul: "Be careful how you live. Don't live like fools, but like those who are wise. Make the most of every opportunity in these evil days. Don't act thoughtlessly, but understand what the Lord wants you to do" (Ephesians 5:15-17). Time is short, so by God's grace, we can keep limping toward growth.

You Can Uncover Your Unreliable Narrator

But what if we aren't perceiving the muddled middle correctly? What if we're telling ourselves the incorrect stories? How do we grow when we've lied to ourselves?

In storytelling, an unreliable narrator is "any narrator who misleads readers, either deliberately or unwittingly. Many are unreliable through circumstances, character flaws or psychological difficulties. In some cases, a narrator withholds key information from readers, or they may deliberately lie or misdirect."[1] We read of the importance of "speak[ing] the truth in love" to our friends and family (Ephesians 4:15), but what if we cannot admit the truth to ourselves?

So what happens when we become unreliable narrators in our own stories?

- *We tend to catastrophize.* In my current season of working through a deep church-hurt wound, I become convinced that I will never get through this—that the muddled middle of healing will never advance and I will always feel sad. Of course, logically I know that that's not true, but it *feels* true. The longer we're in the muddled middle, the stronger the feeling becomes.
- *We can confirm our biases.* Confirmation bias is simply finding things in our environment that confirm our unreliable view. So to use the example above, whenever I see news about Christian leaders falling or harming others, those data points confirm that things in the American church world will never change. Similarly, if I struggle in my job financially, any time there is an economic downturn, it confirms my sad belief that nothing will turn around. This kind of thinking is the antithesis to a restory mindset.
- *We might flat-out believe lies we've been told since childhood.* Words like
  - "you'll never amount to anything" become an albatross narrative that informs and influences our workplaces;

- "you don't matter" cause us to chase after relationships that confirm those horrible words, and we allow ourselves to be continually used or abused;
- "you think you're so cool" create a deep sense of shame and humility; instead of living with healthy self-esteem, we bend over backward to demean ourselves internally and externally;
- "you don't deserve love" subtly sabotage each relationship;
- "you aren't smart" become an obstacle every time we find ourselves in academic settings; and
- "you should not be seen or heard—you're in the way" cause us to shrink back instead of stepping into new adventures (because if we are small, we feel safe).

Unreliable narrators are masters at deception in novels, and in our everyday lives we are often masters at self-deception. The words we've believed feel entirely true because they don't come from nowhere—other people have reinforced them at crucial times in our lives.

To be transparent, I haven't fully figured this out yet. Of course, I try to take every thought captive (2 Corinthians 10:5), but that's not easy to do. I ask the Lord to search my heart. I process with friends or my husband, asking if what I'm believing is true. There's no quick fix for quashing your unreliable narrator. It takes commitment, energy, a good community, and prayer. But I do see that I believe my unreliable narrator less often than I used to, and that's a victory to celebrate.

You Can See Obstacles as a Gift

In the muddled middle, you have the opportunity to learn to see obstacles as gifts, which helps you tell a better and different redemptive story. This, too, is not simple or easy. We know from James 1 that trials produce perseverance. First Peter 1:6-7 reiterates that truth: "Be truly glad. There is wonderful joy ahead, even though you must endure many trials for a little while. These trials will show that your faith is genuine. It is being tested as fire tests and purifies gold—though your faith is far more precious than mere gold. So when your faith remains strong through many trials, it will bring you much praise and glory and honor on the day when Jesus Christ is revealed to the whole world."

I'll be honest: This week I have not been grateful for the trials I'm enduring. My husband's job remains untenable, a health scare has me worried, one of my kids' heartaches has become mine, and I feel harassed by all these things. In times when trials are more of a deluge than a manageable reality, I handle them until I can't.

Are you walking through a season like that right now? You feel capable of handling one obstacle, then another, then another—but when ten obstacles hit you all at once, what can you do? How do you cope? How can you possibly see them as a gift?

I'm not suggesting you should be toxically positive, pretending that traumatic events and frustrating circumstances are easily wrangled. They're not. And we need to acknowledge hard things and grieve them appropriately. It's what comes next that helps turn the tide toward gratitude. Obstacles and trials will not last forever, but their impact will—if we let it. Perhaps that's why Peter instructs us to be "truly glad."

To pursue gratitude, you need to do a bit of excavating of the past. Chances are good that in the past you grew most through the obstacles you encountered. Your faith deepened and your walk with God was strengthened because of those trials. Paradoxically, God uses difficult times to grow us, to cause our roots to sink further into the soil of his love. The better our rooted structures are forged through the storms of life, the higher quality our fruit—our ability to love our enemies, trust God through trials, and find joy even when difficulties arise.

That is why we can thank God for the difficulties of our lives. Because each one comes with a hidden blessing. I've found that the harder the task, the more I really don't want to face something, the more (in retrospect) I learn and grow. I have gotten on my knees just this week, tears in my eyes, saying to the Lord, *Please, please hear me. I don't want this trial. Please make it go away.* But now, after many tears, I have begun to feebly pray, *Okay, Lord, teach me how to glorify you as I endure this trial I'm not happy about.* It's easier to see the blessing in the blight in retrospect, and it's harder to cultivate the discipline of thanking God for the stressor in the moment. This is a deep level of discipleship.

Take note of the juxtaposition of Paul's words to the Philippians: "Dear friends, you always followed my instructions when I was with you. And now that I am away, it is even more important. Work hard to show the results of your salvation, obeying God with deep reverence and fear. For God is working in you, giving you the desire and the power to do what pleases him" (Philippians 2:12-13).

Growing in this way requires hard work. But the latter part of this passage contains a promise—the Lord will give you the power to thank him for the trials. You cannot contrive that on your own. And there is a counterintuitive joy that comes from serving God through our trials. Paul tells us, "I will rejoice even if I lose my life, pouring it out like a liquid offering to God, just like your faithful service is an offering to God. And I want all of you to share that joy. Yes, you should rejoice, and I will share your joy" (Philippians 2:17-18). The quiet of the middle gives us the opportunity to see obstacles and trials as circumstances we pour out for the sake of our God. It is our service of worship—and thankfully, the result is joy.

The restory journey God has us on is one of joy. Is it wearying being stuck in the ambiguity of a waiting season? Absolutely. Is it hard to look back on our stories? Yes. Is it difficult to work through relational difficulties? Of course. Does it take time to reframe obstacles as blessings? Totally. But God's sovereign plan is for our good, for our flourishing—even when we have a hard time discerning that in the moment. These difficult tasks of our discipleship have dividends, thankfully. And the interest compounds beautifully. In John 1, we see tendrils of this promise: "From his abundance we have all received one gracious blessing after another" (John 1:16). We walk on the cobblestones of God's grace, skipping from grace to grace, as we move toward home in this muddled middle.

Restorying the Woman with the Issue of Blood

We are not unlike the woman with the issue of blood, pursuing the healing that Jesus offers, but not quite to the place where our fingers can touch the fringe of his cloak. He is ahead of us, and he is good. He was with us in the past, and he is good. He is holding your hand today amid your mess, and he is good.

The muddled middle will not have the final say.

Questions for Discussion

1. How would you define the muddled middle? What emotions have come with it in your life?
2. Imagine how the woman with the issue of blood must've felt during her stress and sickness. What surprised you about her story? What part of her story encouraged you? Discouraged you?
3. Consider a time when you waited patiently to see what God was doing in a difficult situation. How did you do that?
4. When have you struggled to be patient during an unchanging plot point in your life? Looking back, what lessons shaped your life moving forward?
5. It's hard to see obstacles as a gift. What are some practical ways you can intentionally look for the gifts God may have for you in your obstacles?

[illegible]

[illegible] others and the [illegible]

Self-editing your [illegible]

[illegible] monster, [illegible]

First off, you may try to [illegible] lens of a [illegible] reader, [illegible] and surpass you [illegible] place. [illegible] it, laying out your story [illegible] past [illegible] you [illegible]

The [illegible] different story-structures [illegible] give [illegible] your story upon. [illegible] simplest [illegible] the inverted [illegible] in your life. Just to start [illegible] on, your [illegible] incident you may want to "quickly [illegible] years [illegible] thirteen-year [illegible] highlighting the [illegible] touchstone that shaped [illegible] decades. [illegible] something you want—when you [illegible] you accomplished [illegible] pivot point in your story [illegible] before, then after [illegible] when I was fifteen I had [illegible] Jesus [illegible] I've been living [illegible] working [illegible] to show the results [illegible] with deep [illegible] (Philippians [illegible]) [illegible] my restory [illegible] and to acquire [illegible] healing journ[illegible]

[illegible] you [illegible] in that case, [illegible] shared in the [illegible] beginning. Detail who [illegible] you met along the way when you [illegible] something differen[illegible] what kind of difficulties and [illegible] Did you have a mom[illegible] of profound change? And what does your life look like now that you've learned so much and you're helping others with their restorying?

The chiastic structure may take a little more thought. What wa[illegible]

SIX

Work Through Your Pain Points

We were even promised sufferings. They were part of the programme. We were even told, "Blessed are they that mourn," and I accepted it. I've got nothing that I hadn't bargained for. Of course it is different when the thing happens to oneself, not to others, and in reality, not in imagination.

C. S. LEWIS, *A GRIEF OBSERVED*

Job

I had a good life. Many would have even said it was perfect. Strong, joyful family. Meaningful work. Lacking for nothing. You might say the Almighty smiled upon me then, proclaiming my life good, which surely meant that my heart was good as well. That is what I used to believe. My goodness rewarded by a good God.

But then life hammered me into the ground, pulverizing me to dust. So many tragedies rained down upon my head that I stopped counting them. Instead? I threw dirt on myself, wept, and became so engulfed in my grief that my friends scarcely recognized me.

These friends began well, simply sitting alongside me in my grief. But eventually their advice rankled my ears. Their judgments, too. If only I had been more righteous. If only I recognized my sinful state. If only I had done a thousand things differently, then this fate would not have befallen me. I must've done something horrible to deserve such sadness.

But platitudes rarely assuage the afflicted.

So I turned away from their misplaced words, their attempts to explain the unexplainable. I retreated inward. Grew bewildered and tired and overwhelmed—then angry. I questioned, railed, and doubted.

Before my losses, I had created a life that made logical sense. It felt like something I could control, too. I stayed righteous, and the righteous One showered his blessings upon me. I understood the rules—that if I remained sinless, he would remain faithful. But if I stepped out of bounds . . .

Granted, I know we all bear the scars of the fall of humankind. I know there is an enemy prowling. But in my ignorance, I felt I could make order from the chaos. And for such a long time, my way of viewing the world had been confirmed.

But life is not so simple that formulas work forever. Rules cannot save a soul. And my rules? They became my idols of control. I realize that now, but I did not always.

The Almighty did not seem to mind that I misunderstood his reasoning. But he did have a response to all my angry questions. And his answers leveled me back into the dust again.

Through it all, I realized that while I may have boasted about my connection to the Almighty prior to all these trials, I had not understood him. I had heard of God, known about him, but I had not seen him clearly. But now, after the whirlwind of chastisement, I see God clearly—in splendor, glory, and holiness. I realize that he is God and I am not. I understand his sovereignty over all creatures, not merely me.

And as I prayed for my frustrating counselors, I saw his heart. He is more interested in the tenderness of my heart than my temporary satisfaction. He knows best how to grow me, teach me, bless me, and strengthen me. I may not understand all his ways—and that's the point, isn't it? If I understood all the mysteries, he would be a very small god indeed.

> *I don't wish my story of grief on anyone, but I am a different man now that I've walked through such loss—loss of reputation, health, finances, and most painful of all, people. I may walk with a hitch in my step, but that step makes me deeply empathetic toward anyone who suffers.*
>
> *On the stage of suffering, we are all equals.*

Grief is the common language of our world. It is the atmosphere we breathe, the pollution in our lungs. Sadly, loss is an inevitability of life in a fallen world.

Yesterday in church, I scribbled notes in my sermon notebook as the pastor talked about greed—one of the deadly sins. Had I been greedy? Oh, yes. The week had messed with me in so many ways. I was besieged by my own money mistakes, so much so that I could not find joy. I berated myself for a decision I had made—one that, in the long run, had little bearing on our financial health. But I could not let myself off the hook, so when all those greed verses sprang eloquently from the pastor's mouth, I underlined the words until the line nearly cut through the heft of the paper. Greed, he said, has to do with fear. And I nodded. So much of my own fear revolves around not having enough. I remember those times when I was hungry as a child, when the availability of food was wildly unpredictable, when I would scurry away nuts into crevices of the house just so I would always have a squirrel stash in case the hunger came. To this day I get panicked when there's a line of people waiting to get food. I have an insatiable need to be at the front of the line, the fear is so strong.

The pastor spoke of God's generosity—that the Lord started this whole business in Eden with perfection and extravagance and he ends the story with the same. We will not need sunshine; he will provide it. We will only be completely joyful and satisfied when the new heaven and the new earth come sparkling from heaven like a bride walking down a celestial aisle. This is all true.

But what do we do in the in-between times, when we live in the hulking middle between the *now* and the *not yet*? That's when the pastor said these words: "We are living like orphans."

Tears erupted. I wiped them away. But no amount of wiping could erase the truth of this sentence. As a fatherless girl and the daughter of a mom who, when I was a child, acted as if I were an inconvenience, I had often lived like an orphan, fending for myself, learning to entertain myself as an only child, knowing that I was the only one I could count on to take care of me. No adult was reliable, so I had to become my own adult.

My pain points were predation and then loss, all permeated with a strong sense that I did not matter. And here I was in my fifties in a different denomination, confronting that reality. Living like an orphan.

"But," the pastor finished, "you have a Father who loves you and delights in you."

And tears sprang afresh. But I struggled to believe. Does he?

Have you felt, even in the reading of this book, that everything is up to you? That, even though you know intellectually that God loves you and graces you, every part of your emotional self believes you are unlovable, unseen, and unacknowledged? Do you have that insatiable need to be perfect? To not ever make financial mistakes? To live life in such a way as to prove your sonship or daughtership? Oh, I am living there as I type these words. Because the truth is that all the pain points we experience often shout our unworthiness. They declare our orphanhood.

Pain points define and shape our stories. We, as protagonists, must face them because growth doesn't come from ease of circumstance or earthly nirvana—it comes through the valley of pain.

To recount pain points is to nod our heads to the reality of the fallenness of this world. And the grief that emerges from these pain points can hold us hostage in our frustrating stories, wondering if we will ever truly believe we are loved. Often I have stayed mired in that place, pulled down by grief upon grief.

We are not failures for being broken by pain; we are human. Just recently I read from this book to a group of *Pray Every Day* (my podcast) listeners, recounting my story from chapter 4. It moved one of the women to tears. "I am so broken by your story," she told me.

I am too.

But if I live in that brokenness, I forget that I am made for resurrection. I forget that God, in his infinite kindness, loves me as a father loves his beloved child. I forget that pain cannot negate my belovedness.

Living as orphans is no way to pursue the next chapter of our lives.

Let's look at the life of Job. Let's learn from his story arc. And then let's reach toward Jesus, believing that the journey toward him is worth it.

The Story Arc of Grief

Before we were church planters in France, the neighbors behind us told us that they were walking through foreclosure. I prayed, *Oh Lord, I never, ever want to have to go through that.* For someone like me, who constantly worried about whether I was managing our money well, losing our home was one of my greatest insecurities. Fast-forward eight months to when I found out that we had sold our home in the States to a con man and that we'd be forced to walk through foreclosure. One of my greatest fears had entered my story.

In a broken world, pain is part of every story. And that means that a thread of grief winds its way through our stories as well. Grief isn't just normal; it's necessary. It does us no good to gloss over our pain points, pretending all is well. No, we must work through them, grieve them, feel them, invite God into them. It's not a lack of faith to express your anguish. It's not forbidden to tell God how you feel. He already knows. His desire is to have relationships with us, but if we stuff our emotions and never tell him what's bothering us, we'll miss out on his empathy. Our Savior—he who "was despised and rejected— / a man of sorrows, acquainted with deepest grief" (Isaiah 53:3)—walks alongside us when we grieve.

Job certainly understood the depths of grief and loss, and we can learn much from his life as we work through some of the painful transition points in our lives. When we experienced our foreclosure, I resonated with Job's words after God had allowed Satan, "the prince of the power of the air" (Ephesians 2:2, NKJV), to take everything from Job: "What I always feared has happened to me. / What I dreaded has come true" (Job 3:25). His honest, raw reflections as he mourned gave me language in the early devastating days:

- "Let the day of my birth be erased, / and the night I was conceived" (Job 3:3).
- "Lying in bed, I think, 'When will it be morning?' / But the night drags on, and I toss till dawn" (Job 7:4).
- "I cannot keep from speaking. / I must express my anguish. / My bitter soul must complain" (Job 7:11).
- "My life passes more swiftly than a runner. / It flees away without a glimpse of happiness" (Job 9:25).

Unlike Job, when my pain point hit me, I did not exercise my faith muscle. Instead I worried. I buckled under the pressure. But what I realized, eventually, was that even when I had "perfectly" managed our finances, something out of my control could have ruined everything. Over time I was able to let out my breath and tell the Lord I would trust him through this. Job's words comforted me. His initial faith when his pain points were overwhelming eventually became mine:

"I came naked from my mother's womb,
    and I will be naked when I leave.
The LORD gave me what I had,
    and the LORD has taken it away.
Praise the name of the LORD!"

JOB 1:21

So how can we restory the arc of grief in our own lives? Job's story shows us the way:

bitterness + judgment + loneliness + honesty + sovereignty + acceptance + vindication + forgiveness + restoration + feasting = the story arc of grief

The Story Arc of Grief

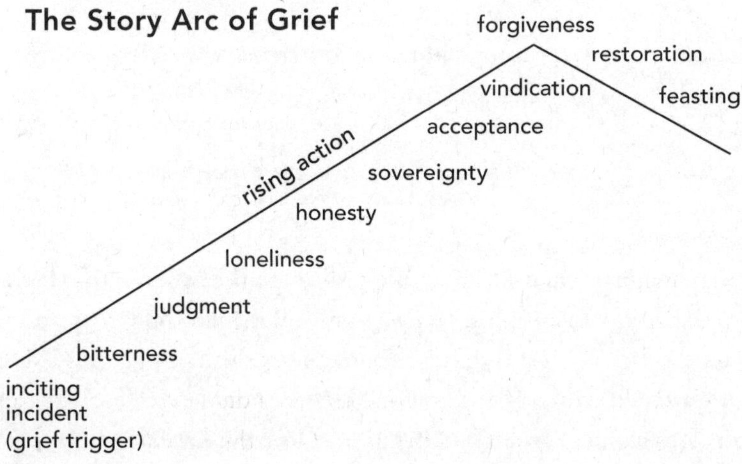

Bitterness

Perhaps you're reluctant to recount your pain points for fear of becoming bitter, worried that shouting them (or writing them out or crying them in prayer) will make your heart brittle. But bitterness actually comes from unexpressed grief. It's a turning inward rather than a reaching outward.

As I write this, my husband and I are in a conflict. We snapped at each other this morning because we are both under a tremendous amount of pressure. We are cooling down. Our pattern in the past has been to give each other the cold shoulder, which is its own form of control and punishment. Perhaps the meanest thing we can do is to isolate ourselves from another person, to stop communication. Today we will, by God's grace, come back to each other, apologize, and move forward. But we cannot do that if we never choose to express our disappointment. It's a simple but frustrating formula:

pain + stuffing it and pretending it doesn't exist = unwanted behavior

But our lives grow through potential bitterness if we adopt a different formula:

pain + expressing it through love to a safe person = growth

Judgment

What happens when we are walking through the valley of the shadow of grief and someone comes along and offers platitudes instead of a listening ear? What if they're a bit unsafe or selfish or uncaring? What if we are met with a friend's self-righteous judgment? Unfortunately, this does happen, and it can derail us. I know it has harmed me.

Job has an interesting way of dealing with this—he first entrusts his pain to God, who is best able to carry the weight of his grief: "My friends scorn me, / but I pour out my tears to God" (Job 16:20). In some of my loneliest times, when my relationships felt unsafe, I learned to holler at the Lord first, knowing he wouldn't break from my honesty—nor would he judge unfairly.

In case you need an example of how *not* to love your friend who is walking through grief, look at this comment from one of Job's friends:

> "Your children must have sinned against him,
> so their punishment was well deserved.
> But if you pray to God
> and seek the favor of the Almighty,
> and if you are pure and live with integrity,
> he will surely rise up and restore your happy home."
>
> JOB 8:4-6

Can you hear the judgment? It oozes out of this uncaring statement. Job's children are deceased! How heartless to level the blame at them. And then the friend attacks Job's integrity, implying he needs to repent. While we always need to ask God to examine our hearts and we should listen to those who love us if they see an errant way in us, during grief we are in a tender place and don't have the capacity to receive heaps of criticism. If you are walking through too many overwhelming pain points to count, be kind to yourself. Surround yourself with kindhearted people who are *for* you, who are unafraid of your tears.

Loneliness

Perhaps the most insidious part of our stories is the loneliness that springs from grief. We feel we are the only ones journeying on this pathway. On a walk today, I told my husband, "I'm just so tired of being sad." He asked me whether I'm depressed. I honestly don't know. But I do know this about myself—in the past few months I have not wanted to be around people. That makes for loneliness, but it's self-imposed. It's harder when you long for community and a settled group of friends is no longer in your life. Job puts it starkly: "My family is gone, / and my close friends have forgotten me" (Job 19:14). So whether you're walking through a season of self-isolation or your friends and family have chosen to isolate from you, you'll have to work through loneliness.

Honesty

As I mentioned earlier, it's important to be honest with the One who created you. His shoulders are big enough to carry what's weighing you down. He welcomes your heart, your worries, your ramblings, your questions. Look at how honest Job is with God:

> "He has thrown me into the mud.
> I'm nothing more than dust and ashes.
>
> "I cry to you, O God, but you don't answer.
> I stand before you, but you don't even look.
> You have become cruel toward me.
> You use your power to persecute me.
> You throw me into the whirlwind
> and destroy me in the storm."
>
> JOB 30:19-22

Have you ever felt like God has become cruel to you? I know someone who is longing to be married. She was brave enough to approach someone who was giving all the right signals and declare her interest (a hard thing to do). She's been praying for over a decade for a husband, and her prayers have often been tear laden but also full of surrender. She has been righteous through this journey. When he said, "I can't see that ever happening," she had to mourn again, and she told the Lord how it made her feel. Her words, I'm sure, echoed Job's.

The truth is, sometimes God seems capricious to us. He, as the Storyteller, holds the beginnings, middles, and endings of our stories, but we don't have such insight. So we walk this bewildering road, wondering why that death happened or that dream died or that health condition won't improve. This is normal. It's okay to question God when you just don't get what he's up to.

This world is broken by sin and selfishness, and sometimes terrible things happen. We can't always make sense of senselessness. But God does see it all. He takes notice of you through the pain. He empathizes with you. He loves you. He knows how to lead you through your darkest seasons, even when you are having a hard time trusting his hand.

Sovereignty

While Job has questioned God about the trials he's walking through, it is only when God turns the questions back on him that resolution begins. God asks the very human Job, "Are you as strong as God? / Can you thunder with a voice like his?" (Job 40:9). Throughout this part of the book of Job, God asks Job impossible questions about the cosmos, how animals behave, and the complexity of creation. Inevitably, when we truly comprehend how large God is and how small we are, whatever pain we face is put into its place under God's sovereignty, his ruling power. God is the Creator of all that we see, all that we experience. He rules over all creation, including us. We cannot know the mysteries and complexities of God, but we can rest in knowing that he is for us—and that, out of his love, he is working behind the scenes to do good to and for us. That's not always easy to discern, and to be honest, some folks have slapped sovereignty on an open grief wound like a Band-Aid to minimize their pain. I wish there were an easy way to balance nihilism ("Nothing matters; who cares") with God's sovereignty ("We matter; God cares").

In your own journey of bewilderment, it's imperative to remind yourself that one member of the sovereign Trinity lives within you. The Holy Spirit is known as a comforter, and he is ever available to you, particularly when questions arise or loneliness threatens to overwhelm you. He will not leave you.

Acceptance

If you've ever been through the Twelve Steps process, you know that acceptance is part of the pathway. Eventually our grief brings us to a place of acceptance. Sometimes that means we must grieve what was, realizing that *what was* is not *what is* and most likely won't be *what will be*. We can only know for sure that change is inevitable. Only our sovereign, immutable God never changes. Job tells the Lord, "I know that you can do anything, / and no one can stop you" (Job 42:2). There is a settled peace that comes when we realize that God is in control and no amount of grief or pain or nefariousness from another can thwart his ways, his plans.

Once we accept the new state of our stories, we then settle into the place where we can experience more of God. Some of the trials I've endured have exposed the ways I used to run to idols to salve my fears. Others have driven me to deeper levels of dependence on God. He is ever at work to refine us, stripping away that which does not profit (though we wrongly think it does). Only when he does can we realize how much we need him in order to survive our stories—and thrive. As I mentioned in the Job monologue at the beginning of this chapter, Job begins his story with everything intact *except* his knowledge of God ("I had heard of God"). In the end, he finally sees the Lord: "I had only heard about you before, / but now I have seen you with my own eyes" (Job 42:5). There's quite a treacherous journey between hearing and seeing. But to see is to experience far more of God than we can by merely hearing of his reputation.

As you look back on your own restory process, have you noticed this journey from hearing to seeing? What has caused you to experience God more? It's not in our times of abundance that we experience his closeness (though he is still there)—it's during our pain points, our griefs, and our sad meanderings where we feel his presence and grow the most.

Vindication

It is never easy to walk through grief. It's not fun to recount pain points. And while we venture through those dark valleys, we are often misunderstood, maligned, and dismissed. Usually when I'm in those places, I don't have enough energy to seek vindication, to right someone's ill opinion of me. I must leave that in God's hands (though I often put my hands back into the mess, desperately trying to micromanage my reputation). At the end of Job's ordeal, God gives him the gift of vindication, basically letting him know he's not crazy. The Lord says to one of Job's "helpful" friends, "I am angry with you and your two friends, for you have not spoken accurately about me, as my servant Job has" (Job 42:7).

When we helped "refugees" from our former church work through their pain in the aftermath of spiritual abuse, the first session we led was called "You Are Not Crazy." Sometimes we just need to know that our perceptions of a problem are not dramatic or inaccurate. The human heart longs for vindication, and how sweet of the Lord to let Job know that, yes, his friends did not act in accordance with God's ways. You may not see vindication immediately, but you can rest in the knowledge that God sees you right now and knows the entire truth of your situation. You can let your reputation rest in his perfect hands.

Forgiveness

In the aftermath of Job's sweet vindication, he experiences restoration, but only after he works through his feelings toward his friends. You know he has done this because of his actions: "Job prayed for his friends" (Job 42:10). In one of my dark days, when I was working through the loss of a friendship, I spent way too much time ruminating about its demise. As I took a deep breath, I decided to pray for my friend instead of rehashing everything and internally protesting my rightness. I prayed that the Lord would set her free and give her the ability to forgive me for her sake, not my own. I prayed for her flourishing. I prayed the Lord would be near her and bless her with his presence. Though I continued to struggle with the aftermath of the relationship, that prayer pivoted my pain point into a turning point. When we can forgive and pray for those who have hurt us, freedom has a way of finding us.

Restoration

If forgiveness is the climax of a story arc, then restoration and feasting are the denouement. God gave back what Job had lost (with, of course, the exception of his lost, irreplaceable children). He exemplified the words the prophet Joel would later speak when he prophesied about God's restoration of Israel after exile:

> The Lord says, "I will give you back what you lost
>   to the swarming locusts, the hopping locusts,
> the stripping locusts, and the cutting locusts.
>   It was I who sent this great destroying army against you.
> Once again you will have all the food you want,
>   and you will praise the Lord your God,
> who does these miracles for you.
>   Never again will my people be disgraced."
>
> JOEL 2:25-26

Notice how similar this story arc is to Job's. God allowed the devastation to come. He permitted Satan to cause calamity. But he also restores what's been devastated. We see this in Job's life as well: "The Lord blessed Job in the second half of his life even more than in the beginning" (Job 42:12).

I would be remiss if I promised you restoration of all pain sources in your life on this earth. I cannot do that. There will always be stories left unfinished. Some aches may wane but still exist nonetheless. However, there will be a day when all things are restored completely. We must fix our eyes on that future: "[Jesus] must remain in heaven until the time for the final restoration of all things, as God promised long ago through his holy prophets" (Acts 3:21).

In reading the following verses from Paul in 2 Corinthians 4:16-18, I am deeply encouraged to think toward that end: "That is why we never give up. Though our bodies are dying, our spirits are being renewed every day. For our present troubles are small and won't last very long. Yet they produce for us a glory that vastly outweighs them and will last forever! So we don't look at the troubles we can see now; rather, we fix our gaze on things that cannot be seen. For the things we see now will soon be gone, but the things we cannot see will last forever."

Restoration is nigh, friend. Your troubles won't last forever. The glory will be worth it. What is unseen will be worth all the pain and grief.

Feasting

At the end of Job's ordeal, we see a feast, a celebration of all God has provided: "Then all his brothers, sisters, and former friends came and feasted with him in his home" (Job 42:11). Similarly, in the nation of Israel's history we see a lot of feasting, each feast held with the purpose of thanking God for what he had provided. Jesus confirmed his power and deity in feasts (for example, the wedding at Cana and the feedings of multitudes). And one day we will all participate in the marriage supper of the Lamb. While sin entered the world through a forbidden feast, it will cease in a welcoming feast for all the tribes of the earth.

Feasting, though, isn't limited to moments when all is finally well. God also allows feasting during relational strife: "You prepare a feast for me / in the presence of my enemies" (Psalm 23:5). It's spiritual warfare to feast in the middle of pain. Consider the great feast in the upper room—even though Jesus was about to be betrayed and the cross loomed ahead of him, he feasted with his friends. This was a precursor to the victory eventually won on Calvary and then through the resurrection. Jesus feasted before and during his suffering. He gives us the power to do so as well.

Honestly, this is one of the tenets of the restoried arc of grief that's hardest for me to practice. I'm a mountain climber but not a summit lingerer. Instead of rejoicing in what God has done, I immediately move on to the next thing without stopping to notice and give God's goodness a second or third thought. I am learning (slowly) how important it is to stop to celebrate God's goodness, to slow down long enough to enjoy the restorying that God has done in my life.

Restorying Job

Where do you find yourself in the restoried arc of grief? When have you experienced the kinds of losses Job faced? What bitterness do you need to surrender today? How have you experienced others' judgment and pat answers, and how did that affect your heart? Where are you on the loneliness scale as you tackle your grief? What needs to be unlearned for you to be truly honest with God about your grief? How does God's sovereignty help you navigate what is next? Have you come to a place of settled acceptance? While vindication can be fickle, have you seen little snapshots of it in your life right now? How is your forgiveness journey turning out? What has God restored in your life through your grief journey? What victories need to be celebrated by feasting? Asking these questions will help us understand where we are on the restory arc of grief—and empower us to move forward in our dynamic stories.

When our pain points receive God's restorying power, we can sing along with the psalmists, who remind us that God is in this journey alongside us:

> What joy for those who can live in your house,
> always singing your praises.

What joy for those whose strength comes from the Lord,
 who have set their minds on a pilgrimage to Jerusalem.
When they walk through the Valley of Weeping,
 it will become a place of refreshing springs.
 The autumn rains will clothe it with blessings.
They will continue to grow stronger,
 and each of them will appear before God in Jerusalem.

O Lord God of Heaven's Armies, hear my prayer.
 Listen, O God of Jacob.

PSALM 84:4-8

May the Lord hear your prayers as you navigate the pain points in your story, friend. And may you see his goodness even today as you read these words.

Questions for Discussion

1. What do you most connect with in Job's arc of grief? What doesn't seem related to your current season?
2. What did you learn about Job from this chapter? How did he change from before his trials to afterward?
3. Recall a recent pain point in your life. What happened? Did you find helpful people to walk with you? Or did you experience platitudes and judgment like Job did?
4. When have you struggled to forgive someone during your grief? What happened? What has the forgiveness journey looked like for you?
5. Do you struggle with feasting? With celebrating when life slows down and your circumstances are good? Why or why not?

of profound change, and what does your life look like now that you've learned so much and you're helping others with their restorying?

The chiastic structure may take a little more thought. What wa

SEVEN

Discover the *So What?* of Your Story

In the first act you get your hero up a tree.
The second act, you throw rocks at him.
For the third act you let him down.
ATTRIBUTED TO GEORGE ABBOTT, THEATER PRODUCER AND DIRECTOR

The Ethiopian Eunuch

The journey from Ethiopia to Jerusalem had been arduous and hot, and I found myself quite weary as I retraced my pathway back toward home. To have represented Candace, my queen, in that beautiful city—the place that was supposed to be the home of the King of heaven, the Lord of lords—was my supreme privilege. She had entrusted her treasuries to me, giving me the title of court official. She is the one I represented in the journey toward worship.

I did not know the intricacies of worship, but the Temple, which sat in the belly of that high city, gleamed like one of Candace's jewels. I found myself caught up in the revelry—and yet something felt amiss, though I could not put my finger on it at the time.

Grateful for Candace's chariot as transport when the sun beat down upon the canopy above me, I puzzled over the parchment scroll in front of me. The words blurred as I tried to make sense of them. Something about sheep and a great slaughter. What could this bloodied passage mean?

And how did it tie into the spectacle of the Temple I had just experienced? I read the words out loud, hoping that by doing so I would gain more understanding, but none came. Still, I persisted.

A man—named Philip, I would soon learn—approached me from the left side of the chariot. He seemed friendly. "Do you understand what you are reading?" he said.

I let out a sigh. "How can I, unless someone instructs me?"

The man had a glowing look about him. Something inside me felt he could be trusted, so I invited him to join me in the chariot.

"Sit beside me," I told him. The horses carried us away toward my homeland as the wheels navigated the rutted road.

"What passage are you reading?" the man named Philip asked.

I pointed to the page, then began reading out loud: "He was led like a sheep to the slaughter. And as a lamb is silent before the shearers, he did not open his mouth. He was humiliated and received no justice. Who can speak of his descendants? For his life was taken from the earth." I turned to Philip. "Tell me," I asked, "was the prophet talking about himself or someone else?"

Philip smiled. "Someone else—the Son of God." And then he spoke of a man named Jesus, whom he also called the Christ—how he lived a life of miracles on this earth, healing many, feeding the poor, expelling demons from tortured souls, and proclaiming a brand-new Kingdom come to earth. He spoke of a deep betrayal by a close friend, the religious leaders' triumph, and punishment on the Roman cross. So enraptured was I in the story that I wept when I heard it. Surely the passage I had been reading was about this Jesus of Nazareth. And his life had been snuffed out.

"He is dead," I said to the canopy of the sky. My soul mourned.

"No," Philip said.

"No?"

"No, on the third day after his crucifixion, Jesus rose from the dead and appeared to many. He is alive!"

This felt like far too much to take in. How could a dead person breathe our air again? It would be like me becoming whole again, able to father children. It simply could not happen.

As if reading my thoughts, Philip said, "It really did happen. And that is the good news. Anyone who believes in Jesus and is baptized will have eternal life!"

I wanted this more than anything—even more than all the status Queen Candace had afforded me. It was then I saw the pond to our left. "Look! There's some water!" I called out. "Why can't I be baptized?"

I told the carriage to stop, and we dismounted together. Philip asked me if I believed this incredible story about Jesus, and all at once all that confusion I'd experienced in Jerusalem faded into peace. "I do. I believe Jesus is the Son of the only God in heaven. I believe he died and then conquered death by rising again."

He gently pushed me into the water. Its coolness salved my fatigued body. For that moment beneath the surface of the waters, I nearly panicked. It felt a bit like death, and suddenly I understood: In an infinitesimal way, I was identifying with the death of God's Son. Who I was before this moment took pause. As the water rushed past me and my mouth tasted air, I felt awakened. I was dead before this journey, a eunuch with no vitality, but now I am alive to the most beautiful story ever told. I looked to my left and right to thank Philip, my companion in a newfound faith—but to my astonishment, he had disappeared. I asked the chariot driver what he had seen, and he told me that the man had simply evaporated before his eyes.

It was only later that I learned that an angel had told Philip to go to that deserted place. It makes the encounter even more unbelievable, if I am honest.

Friend, there is a *So what?* to your story. The *So what?* is what storytellers call the climax of every story, the moment when the main character discovers why they've faced all that stress, all those pain points. It's the *aha*, the "I get it now." It's what makes the story make sense. Without a climax, a reader is left in suspended animation, still waiting for the story to be resolved.

The climax each of us experiences in our individual story involves our encounter with the gospel. Our lives hinge on it. When I recount my story, there is a *before Jesus* and an *after Jesus*. Who I was prior to meeting Jesus? She is gone. Paul puts it starkly: "My old self has been crucified with Christ. It is no longer I who live, but Christ lives in me. So I live in this earthly body by trusting in the Son of God, who loved me and gave himself for me" (Galatians 2:20). The hinge point is always love. It's Jesus' sacrifice. It's transformation.

For the Ethiopian eunuch, Jesus' miraculous transformation of his heart became the platform by which he spread the gospel to many in his context.[1] And his is a particularly poignant story because he symbolizes the great reversal. Isaiah 56:3-5 shows us just how thorough God's redemption is. Isaiah prophesies,

> "Don't let foreigners who commit themselves to the LORD say,
>   'The LORD will never let me be part of his people.'
> And don't let the eunuchs say,
>   'I'm a dried-up tree with no children and no future.'

> For this is what the Lord says:
> I will bless those eunuchs
> who keep my Sabbath days holy
> and who choose to do what pleases me
> and commit their lives to me.
> I will give them—within the walls of my house—
> a memorial and a name
> far greater than sons and daughters could give.
> For the name I give them is an everlasting one.
> It will never disappear!"

Philip witnessed the fulfillment of this prophecy in real time, and it's recorded in the Word of God for all of us. No matter how broken you feel you are, no matter how fallow or unfruitful, whether you feel outcast or invisible, the truth remains: Jesus loves you and has a future prepared for you that is far more glorious than you can imagine.

These gifts begin at the climax (meeting Jesus), but blessing does not end there. The rest of our lives are an exercise of becoming whole and practicing wholehearted devotion to the One who brought a great reversal in our lives. We once were lost, but now we are truly found.[2]

In Pursuit of Holy Optimism

After the eunuch's interaction with Philip, the Scripture says this: "The eunuch never saw him again but went on his way rejoicing" (Acts 8:39). To rejoice is to acknowledge the power of God in your life and to marvel at all he has done—to never forget this new, beautifully altered life.

I am bothered by the words to the church in Ephesus in Revelation 2:

> "I know all the things you do. I have seen your hard work and your patient endurance. I know you don't tolerate evil people. You have examined the claims of those who say they

> are apostles but are not. You have discovered they are liars. You have patiently suffered for me without quitting.
>
> "But I have this complaint against you. You don't love me or each other as you did at first! Look how far you have fallen! Turn back to me and do the works you did at first. If you don't repent, I will come and remove your lampstand from its place among the churches."
>
> REVELATION 2:2-5

The church began well. They experienced the climax of their story in meeting Jesus, then they worked very hard. They exposed hypocrisy and heresy. They suffered and endured. But they lost the zeal of their first love. Their rejoicing waned.

While it's not sustainable to live in a constant state of Pollyanna bliss, there is something to be said for holy optimism, for hearkening back to that climactic moment when we first encountered Jesus Christ. To remember our first love. To fight against cynicism. That is not an easy endeavor, particularly when you've faced trials stacked on trials.

The apostle Paul faced hardships throughout his ministry life, and he summarizes some of his angst and worry in 2 Corinthians 11, where he writes of beatings, persecutions, and far too many trials. He concludes by using positive language, boasting, "If I must boast, I would rather boast about the things that show how weak I am. God, the Father of our Lord Jesus, who is worthy of eternal praise, knows I am not lying. When I was in Damascus, the governor under King Aretas kept guards at the city gates to catch me. I had to be lowered in a basket through a window in the city wall to escape from him" (2 Corinthians 11:30-33). Note that he doesn't underplay the trials. Paul is unfailingly honest, but he finds a way to work through his challenging circumstances by realizing that his weakness is the invitation to God's powerful strength. This marriage of the two attributes (weakness plus strength) reveals Paul's genuine first love. He knows he cannot endure without the help of his Savior.

The Redemption in Your *So What?*

If you are a Christ follower, the climax of your story has a *before* and an *after*. This is true whether you met Jesus as a child or through a slow process or in a radical way. But sharing the same *So what?* doesn't mean that our stories are all the same. Here's the truth: Our unique beginnings, contexts, pain points, and inciting incidents weave together redemptive threads that God intended just for us. And as we mine the depths of our narratives, we begin to uncover clues to our callings.

How can we figure out the *So what?*s of our stories? It's not easy, particularly if we only look at our lives as we look inward. We need others to help us. When I found myself walking through a discernment process about my purpose and vocation—a process that, incidentally, ended up in the *restory* messaging, the first thing I did was poll my friends and family. I asked,

- "What adjective or verb do you think of when you think of me?"
- "What is the one thing I do that helps other people?"
- "What am I uniquely gifted to do?"
- "How has my story helped you in your story?"

Their answers were life-changing, and I don't say that lightly. Words like *freedom*, *joy*, *connection*, *empathy*, and *encouraging* sprouted up. (It was a salve to my soul to read those!) When it came to how I help others, *emancipation* came up. I help people be set free from their pasts. Others said I am uniquely gifted to be authentic—to tell stories about myself so that others feel less alone.

I would not have discovered this about myself through mere introspection. I needed my brothers and sisters to see me, to help me discern who I am and how I help others heal.

It may seem terrifying to you to ask such things. But you don't have to start on a global scale. Just ask a friend one of these questions, and then listen to their response. Sometimes we can't see the beauty in ourselves, though it is obvious to others.

Finding your *So what?* may involve a quest. You may have to look through your story to find a redemptive thread, which will be there even when redemption seems impossible. When it comes to one particular character in my story—my biological father—this has not been an easy or straightforward task. For a long time I lionized my father, imagining him with all sorts of heroic qualities. This is easy for a young child to do when they lose a parent. It was only later that I began to see how he had groomed me from an early age. Had he lived, I know I would have become the victim of something more far-reaching and depraved than what I was exposed to.

As I dug deeper into his life, I kept finding more frightening rabbit trails leading to newer levels of depravity. For a long time I despised my father, though I fought to forgive him. It's both hard and easy to pardon a dead perpetrator, I have found. Eventually, as I mentioned earlier, I simply had to land on not truly understanding him. I wasn't meant to. No matter how many investigations I did, each layer of sin only smelled more like a stench. Though I could admit that he was a human being in need of love and forgiveness, I also had to come to terms with the fact that I would never tie him up in a neat testimony package.

For a long time I could not find a redemptive thread running through this train wreck of a story. How do you reconcile that your father was a sexual perpetrator, a narcissistic sociopath with psychopathic tendencies? How does that fit into a story of redemption?

It doesn't.

At least not on the surface. This restory has taken years to unearth.

You see, I am a writer, and he was a writer—a far better one than I'll ever be.

I am an artist, and he was a photographer—a far better one than I'll ever be.

His creativity flows through me—*but God has redeemed it.* God has taken what caused my father's deepest forays into evil (pornography in both realms) and transformed them into prose and art for the Kingdom of God. I am deeply humbled by the discovery, the most powerful restory I've experienced. My vocation goes far deeper than a spiritual-gifts inventory—it's the coded part of my soul, the way God knit me in my mother's womb, the way I process pain. As I look back on my life, I realize that a lot of profound healing has happened through this gift God has given me.

Let that sink in. *The gifts God has given you are the shape of your redemption.* He uses the unique makeup of each one of us to bring healing to our hearts through the power of the Spirit within. You may have heard of spiritual pathways—those ways we connect to God. (There are many lists, but common ones include worship, nature, solitude, study, community, and service.) But what about healing pathways? One of the ways God heals you is through how he has created you. Your story restories you. Your personality and gifts are things God uses to bring you to wholeness. Once you meet Jesus at the climax of your story, you have a new mind to consider the ways he will (slowly and gently) shape your healing journey to the dimensions of your soul.

If the Lord had shown me at the outset all I would have faced in my healing journey, I would have run clear away. I certainly would not have predicted that in my quest for healing I'd write dozens of books. Or paint hundreds of pictures. Or sing thousands of songs. Or speak to many, many people on and off stages. All these creative endeavors were God's Mary-shaped way of helping me heal.

What about you?

How has God gifted you?

What makes you stand out from others?

What is unique in your story that no one else has?

How have your trials informed your triumphs?

What has God uncaged you from?

How have you been set free?

How is your healing journey different from your friends' or your family members'?

There is no formula for discerning these unique healing pathways; it's more of an investigative—yet joyful—journey of discovery.

Remember, if this is hard to discern, ask a friend. Their words may just unstick you.

When I realized that God used some of my father's gifts within me to bring me boatloads of healing, I had a greater appreciation for the story-weaving capabilities of the Lord. He can take what the enemy of our souls meant for our demise and utterly transform us for the better. How can that be? It again causes me to remember God as my first love, the One who can create beauty from chaos.

I cannot recount how many times I cried out to God, trying to make sense of my story. Sometimes he was silent. But even in that holy quiet he was working. You see this kind of longing and fulfillment in David's cry for help: "Hear me, Lord, and have mercy on me. / Help me, O Lord" (Psalm 30:10). Do you relate? But look at what happens after his outreach of longing: "You have turned my mourning into joyful dancing. / You have taken away my clothes of mourning and clothed me with joy, / that I might sing praises to you and not be silent. / O Lord my God, I will give you thanks forever!" (Psalm 30:11-12). From graveclothes to dance outfits, from weeping to praising. When we meet Jesus in the climaxes of our stories, these possibilities begin—and they are shaped just like us. He doesn't redeem us into different people—he makes us the healed versions of ourselves. We become more like ourselves every day on this powerful healing journey.

Pivot from You to Them

After the climax of your story, you can pivot from mining your own story toward becoming passionately interested in the stories of others. Our *So what?*s often stretch beyond our own stories into the stories of others. Before meeting Jesus, I lived in my head—something quite easy to do for an only child—but when I met Jesus, a new group of friends opened up to me, and I began caring for their needs and struggles. The Scriptures are clear that once we are dynamically changed by Jesus, a shift toward sacrificial service occurs. We are restoried to help others find new stories. Consider these powerful verses:

- *We sacrifice ourselves for the needs of others:* "'I was hungry, and you fed me. I was thirsty, and you gave me a drink. I was a stranger, and you invited me into your home. I was naked, and you gave me clothing. I was sick, and you cared for me. I was in prison, and you visited me'" (Matthew 25:35-36).
- *We consider service a privilege:* "'Even the Son of Man came not to be served but to serve others and to give his life as a ransom for many'" (Mark 10:45).
- *We understand how joyful it is to give:* "'I have been a constant example of how you can help those in need by working hard. You should remember the words of the Lord Jesus: "It is more blessed to give than to receive"'" (Acts 20:35).
- *We delight in serving others:* "Love each other with genuine affection, and take delight in honoring each other" (Romans 12:10).
- *Freedom informs our service:* "You have been called to live in freedom, my brothers and sisters. But don't use your freedom to satisfy your sinful nature. Instead, use your freedom to serve one another in love" (Galatians 5:13).

- *We understand that helping others is what Jesus would do. We follow his example:* "Don't look out only for your own interests, but take an interest in others, too" (Philippians 2:4).
- *We serve because we understand God's justice:* "God is not unjust. He will not forget how hard you have worked for him and how you have shown your love to him by caring for other believers, as you still do" (Hebrews 6:10).

While it is important to be retrospective and introspective when we look at our own stories, eventually we—due to the Holy Spirit empowering us—won't be able to help but look for the needs of others. And that's the most powerful part of being restoried.

- We are blessed to be a blessing.
- We are healed to become healers.
- We are graced to demonstrate grace to many.
- We are transformed to become agents of transformation.
- We are empowered so we can cheer on the power we see in others.
- We are loved so we can shower others with unconditional love.
- We are given hope so we can instill hope in others.
- We are forgiven so we can become forgivers.
- We are settled so we can help others find peace.
- We are restoried so we can play a part in other people's restory journeys.

Restorying the Ethiopian Eunuch

The Ethiopian eunuch began his journey empty in many ways, but he ended his story with a flourish—a baptism that marked his journey from unbelief to belief. I would imagine that he'd had no speculation that that day would utterly transform his life through a divine encounter. Similarly, I love how often I've anticipated the mundane only to be surprised by God's surprising intervention. In a moment our lives can be changed—and living in holy expectation of God's ability to do something new is a terrific way to walk our journeys.

God is able to take our everyday stories and fashion entirely new things from the seeds of the past. When we meet Jesus, he sets in motion an adventure of joyful spirituality, personal healing, relational connection, and community participation, despite our wounds and current preoccupations. The paradoxical Kingdom of God means God takes itty-bitty mustard seeds and makes trees, fashions molehills that morph into mountains, woos spores of yeast to create fully raised loaves, and can use five loaves and two fish to make a feast for thousands. As Jesus transforms us, we become his hands and feet to a world in desperate need of his love and light.

Questions for Discussion

1. How has knowing Jesus shaped the *So what?* of your story? What ministry has arisen from your past misery?
2. What redemptive threads have you noticed God weaving through your story?
3. How did God restory the Ethiopian eunuch?
4. As you look back on your life, what do you see as its most pivotal point? Why?
5. Who has helped you discern why God placed you here on this earth? How have they encouraged you to live a new story?
6. What people do you most love to serve?

[illegible] which we push [illegible]

[illegible]

Self-editing your [illegible]

[illegible]

In short, you may try [illegible]

[illegible] your story upon. [illegible] simple [illegible] ("inverted"), one [illegible] of place, [illegible] in your life. Just to [illegible] "chunk" [illegible] fifteen-year [illegible] highlighting the [illegible] decades. [illegible] any time you want—when you [illegible] your children, or that [illegible] pivot point to your story [illegible] before, then after. [illegible] one to fifteen [illegible] working [illegible] with deep [illegible] restory [illegible] healing journ[illegible]

[illegible] In that case, [illegible] in the di[illegible] beginning. Detail who you met along the way, when you [illegible] something different, what kind of [illegible] you learn. Did you have a mom[illegible] of profound change? And what does your life look like now that you've learned so much and you're helping others with their restorying?

The chiastic structure may take a little more thought. What was the main pivot [illegible]

EIGHT

Walk Out Your Story

I have fought the good fight, I have finished the race, and I have remained faithful.

PAUL, 2 TIMOTHY 4:7

Rahab

I did not see them at first—the spies. But I'd heard rumors—so many tales of their god's escapades and prowess. The stories had caused me to pause and worry. If this god wanted our Jericho land, he would have it, and I would not be able to escape his clutches.

Though I only knew Jehovah by reputation, I began talking to him in the quiet of the evenings as I paced the rooftop. So keen was my worry that my dialogue ran for hours, though I could not be sure if a god such as this would listen to me. Particularly because of the way I had to make ends meet in this walled city. Hungry men paid well to have their fleeting appetites whetted. But every time I gathered new coins, I felt a bit of my soul rip from me.

When the men knocked upon my door and I opened it to see them dusted by a long journey, I knew these two would either be the death or the life of me. I soon learned they did not want my services. Instead they needed shelter. So I chose to offer them protection in hopes that an exchange would be made, one that would rescue me from my life.

When my countrymen demanded I bring out the two Israelite spies—a king's decree, no less—I defied their orders. "Yes, the men were here earlier," I told them, "but I didn't know where they were from. They left the town at dusk, as the gates were about to close. I don't know where they went. If you hurry, you can probably catch up with them." Did my lies justify saving human lives? What does this god require of me? Will he reward me for this transgression—or am I doomed to the fate of my fellow citizens?

I told the spies to swear an oath that I would be protected, alongside my family, when they sounded the call to attack. All I wanted was life.

They pledged their own lives, guaranteeing my safety with two catches: I could not betray them at any time, and I had to thrust a scarlet rope from my upper roof, the very rooftop they escaped from, as a sign.

Fear strangled my countrymen—they had barred entry to our city because the Israelites camped within eyeshot of our great walls, in which we trusted. When they began a seven-day march around its perimeter, the terror increased. I kept my family close, confined in the safety of the walls of my home. I did not want my story, or theirs, to end in tragedy.

So we waited each day as the amalgamation of people walked silently around our homeland. On the final day, horns blew, shouts erupted, and our walls buckled beneath the terror. Yet my home remained intact. To my relief, the spies kept their promise, removed us safely from our home—my father and mother, my brothers, and the remaining relatives I had convinced to stay with me. They escorted us to a safe place. Only then did I turn and see my home up in smoke, ashes snowing the air. Though grateful, I felt my life was over.

But the god who frightened me for his ferocity and power soon became my God as I grieved. His reversal was swift—I married into the nation, becoming the wife of Salmon, and then bore him a son, Boaz.

From fearful outcast to invited wife.
From a pagan nation to a God-fearing one.
From prostitute to matron.
From dreamless to dreams fulfilled.
From unknown to known.
From used to loved.

Rahab's story does not end at her rescue and marriage and motherhood. If you read her narrative throughout the Bible, you see that her son, Boaz, also married a foreigner, Ruth, who gave birth to Obed, who fathered Jesse, who fathered King David—a family line that eventually led to the birth of Jesus. (You can read this in Matthew 1.) She is praised for her faith in Hebrews 11:31—"It was by faith that Rahab the prostitute was not destroyed with the people in her city who refused to obey God. For she had given a friendly welcome to the spies"—and again in James 2:25: "Rahab the prostitute is another example. She was shown to be right with God by her actions when she hid those messengers and sent them safely away by a different road." Her restory began with faith, and it ended up in a heroic bloodline reaching all the way to the Messiah. She was not part of the nation of Israel initially, yet God grafted her in—like her future daughter-in-law, Ruth—beautifully.

We, too, if we are Gentiles by birth, are like Rahab. Paul writes, "Some of these branches from Abraham's tree—some of the people of Israel—have been broken off. And you Gentiles, who were branches from a wild olive tree, have been grafted in. So now you also receive the blessing God has promised Abraham and his children, sharing in the rich nourishment from the root of God's special olive tree" (Romans 11:17).

As outsiders, we have been grafted to the rootstock of the Lord, thanks to Jesus and his victory over sin on the cross. We can now be part of "God's special olive tree" as we live out the denouements of our lives.

What Comes Next

What happens after the climax of your story? Your story enters the journey of sanctification. That word simply means "the action or process of being freed from sin or purified."[1]

While it can be daunting to think about the arduous task of becoming clean, it's actually the most joyful journey you can take. When you are restoried by Jesus, you are called to do something new. After Paul reminds us of the importance of working out our salvation, he writes, "Do everything without complaining and arguing, so that no one can criticize you. Live clean, innocent lives as children of God, shining like bright lights in a world full of crooked and perverse people" (Philippians 2:14-15).

The process of sanctification is one full of light and freedom. Discipleship, becoming like Jesus, is where our desire for him meets his ability to transform us.

This is where the rubber meets the road of our faith. The denouement is beckoning, not with rules or God's wrath or exhausting ourselves with our "try" muscles but with grace and strength. We cannot manufacture cleanness, but Jesus grants it. We cannot free ourselves, but Jesus is our Emancipator. We cannot grow in Christ through our own efforts, but when our weakness is bonded to his inner power, growth can't help but occur. That's why Jesus spoke so eloquently of staying connected to him in the upper room discourse. He warns and beckons his disciples with these words:

> "Remain in me, and I will remain in you. For a branch cannot produce fruit if it is severed from the vine, and you cannot be fruitful unless you remain in me.
>
> "Yes, I am the vine; you are the branches. Those who remain in me, and I in them, will produce much fruit. For apart from me you can do nothing."
>
> JOHN 15:4-5

Many translations use the word *abide* instead of *remain*. What does it mean to abide?

> "Abide" is a translation of the Greek word [*menō*]. This word has a range of possible translations, including: to remain, to stay, to lodge with, to wait for, to keep on, to continue to exist, to persist, to reside, to tarry, to stand fast, to stand firm in battle.
>
> Abiding is active. To abide in love means to persist in love, to stand fast in love, to stay put in love. It's a firm commitment.[2]

Simply put, remaining connected to Jesus is an act of persistence, a longing to remain connected to him, come what may.

Why is this so vital? Because we become the people we hang out with. Investor Warren Buffett says, "It pays to hang around with people better than you are because you will float upward a little bit. And if you hang around with people that behave worse than you, pretty soon you'll start sliding down the pole. It just works that way."[3]

While this is a good life lesson in choosing your friends wisely, a restoried life requires hanging out with, remaining in, abiding with Jesus Christ. We cannot be transformed by him if we avoid him—just as a mentee cannot glean much of anything by ignoring their mentor.

In college, I wanted to be connected to the Lord so much that these words became my heartbeat: "Search for the Lord and for his strength; / continually seek him" (1 Chronicles 16:11). Scripture tells us that we really have only two mandates in the denouement of our lives: to love Jesus with everything inside us and then to love with lavish abandon the people he has created (Matthew 22:37-39).

But how do we do that exactly? How do we abide with Jesus?

Pray

We tend to think of prayer as stale, lofty, or impossible—but it is simply talking to God about what you encounter throughout the day. In the classic book *The Practice of the Presence of God*, Brother Lawrence exemplifies the moment-by-moment conversation of abiding with Jesus: "God does not ask much of you. But remembering Him, praising Him, asking for His grace, offering Him your troubles, or thanking Him for what He has given you will console you all the time. During your meals or during any daily duty, lift up your heart to Him, because even the least little remembrance will please Him. You don't have to pray out loud; He's nearer than you can imagine."[4]

Madame Guyon, a postmedieval French prayer warrior who was imprisoned by the Catholic Church after she published *A Short and Very Easy Method of Prayer*, says that while prayer is not merely about us telling God things, it is his nature and desire to overly reciprocate, to give back to us far more than we seek: "I have found it easy to obtain the presence of God. He desires to be more present to us than we are to seek Him. He desires to give Himself to us far more readily than we are to receive Him. We only need to know *how* to seek God, and this is easier and more natural than breathing."[5]

We can pray silently. But sometimes we must voice our prayers. During a recent health stress (which was also compounded by money issues, job insecurity, church pain, and reputation attacks), I stopped everything and grabbed Patrick's hand. "I need to pray," I told him. For whatever reason, just keeping prayer inside me did nothing to quell my worries. Instead, voicing every single stress point calmed me. I'll probably end up being one of those women in nursing homes who talks to herself, only I'll be praying out loud to Jesus for the whole "congregation" to hear.

Be Quiet

Our cacophonous world is getting more persistently noisy every day. Not a moment goes by without us being bombarded by advertisements and hype or gloom and doom and fake news. It's enough to overwhelm us and keep us tethered to stress. And yet the Scriptures teach us much about the importance of quietness and solitude:

- *God is not found in the rancor but in the quietness of whispers.* "After the earthquake there was a fire, but the LORD was not in the fire. And after the fire there was the sound of a gentle whisper" (1 Kings 19:12).
- *God instructs us in quiet places.* "'Teach me, and I will keep quiet. / Show me what I have done wrong'" (Job 6:24).
- *We are strengthened in times of quiet retreat.* "This is what the Sovereign LORD, / the Holy One of Israel, says: / 'Only in returning to me / and resting in me will you be saved. / In quietness and confidence is your strength. / But you would have none of it'" (Isaiah 30:15).
- *In being quiet, we enlarge our capacity to receive God's deliverance.* "It is good to wait quietly / for salvation from the LORD" (Lamentations 3:26).

- *When we are quiet, we are emulating Jesus.* "Before daybreak the next morning, Jesus got up and went out to an isolated place to pray" (Mark 1:35).
- *Much of life is quiet, unflashy obedience.* "Make it your goal to live a quiet life, minding your own business and working with your hands, just as we instructed you before" (1 Thessalonians 4:11).

If we want restoried lives that reflect God's countercultural Kingdom, we must look at the patterns of this world and seek a different direction. Solitude and silence are radical practices because both allow us to hear the still, small voice of God. According to Romans 12:1-2, we are to retrain our minds, letting God transform us, proving what his will is. That's the only way we won't be conformed to our chaotic and noisy world.

Read Scripture

What better way to get to know our God than to read the words he penned through others? These days, sadly, the Bible is often a neglected book. Being ignorant of its nuance and story arc can cause us not to question or weigh what we hear from the pulpit or on YouTube or Instagram. We become far more interested in consuming regurgitated content than going to the source itself. A friend of mine told me about her pastor (since fired) who plagiarized nearly all his sermons. Since they represented the hard work of another, they sounded biblical and catchy. But because he didn't do the work of going directly to the Scriptures himself, he was inadvertently training his congregation to do the same. We should not be spiritual cows, chewing the cud of other people's sermonized words. We must graze on the Word of God ourselves, gleaning wisdom through hard-won study and wrestling.

I encourage you, at least once in your life, to read the Bible through rapidly. This practice has completely transformed my life, more than any other spiritual practice.[6] It's where I began to make connections throughout the Word of God, seeing God's redemptive story throughout the Law, the Prophets, and the New Testament. Reading the whole narrative of Scripture in one truncated period

- allows you to see themes, common narratives, wisdom, and the consequences of sin and selfishness;
- empowers you to discern truth from error; and
- causes you to realize the part you play in God's redemptive story.

Your foundation in Christ will become stronger as you understand his life in the context of the entire narrative of Scripture.

Explore the Spiritual Disciplines

Beyond the three granddaddies of spiritual disciplines we've just explored, there are many spiritual practices we can adopt that will help us know and love Jesus more and more. Paul recommends that Timothy not "waste time arguing over godless ideas and old wives' tales. Instead, train yourself to be godly" (1 Timothy 4:7). No one really loves the idea of discipline, but it's a necessary pursuit as we walk out our sanctification restorying. Here are a few disciplines you might like to explore:

- **Confession.** Letting God know you recognize your sin and asking him to forgive you is the first step toward a surrendered life. As often as we confess our sins to him and to each other, we experience his radical forgiveness.

- **Fasting.** Abstaining from food or media or whatever it is that holds you captive is a good way to reorient your heart toward the Lord and his desires for you.

- **Generosity.** Sometimes it's our tight hold of control and finances and time that causes us to stray and not experience God's flourishing. The disciplines of giving and stewardship help us remind ourselves that the Lord owns everything and is our provider.

- **Gratitude.** I don't tend toward gratitude—I slip into pessimism quite naturally. To reframe my difficult story, I've learned (slowly) that I experience God as I thank him for what he is doing, what he has given me, and the beauty of the world around me. When I seek to be grateful, I live with holy expectation of what the Lord will do. That's a far more interesting and adventurous way to live.

- **Hiddenness.** God rewards those who do things behind the scenes—not for our glory or recognition but for the sake of his Kingdom and glory. Note how Jesus puts it in the Sermon on the Mount: "When you do a charitable deed, do not let your left hand know what your right hand is doing, that your charitable deed may be in secret; and your Father who sees in secret will Himself reward you openly" (Matthew 6:3-4, NKJV). There is much joy in knowing that Jesus sees the good deeds you hide from the world.

- **Journaling.** I frequently share the deepest parts of my heart and longings with the Lord through the written word. Often I am tangled up inside and the only way to detangle is to write everything down. Journaling isn't for everyone, but this discipline has helped me connect with the Lord, particularly when I'm stressed. Another practice you can use alongside journaling is the monastic practice of examen, where you prayerfully use writing to reflect on the day:

- *Gratitude:* What worked well?
- *Petition:* What was difficult?
- *Review:* What were the plot points of the day?
- *Forgiveness:* Whom do you need to pardon?
- *Renewal:* Where did you see light?

- **Lectio divina.** This ancient monastic practice is quite rudimentary: read, reflect, respond, rest. You read a passage of the Bible out loud slowly. Then you quiet yourself and reflect on its words. Then you read it again—the same passage—asking God to show you insights into the words. This reading is like reflective prayer. After that you rest, asking the Lord to keep reminding you of what you've learned.

- **Sabbath.** Taking a day off every week not only helps reset your soul but also gives you space to encounter the One who created it.

- **Scripture memory.** Committing the Word of God to memory has benefits in the moment, but it also pays dividends in the future. I still remember verses I memorized thirty years ago—they pop into my mind when I'm teaching or facing a difficult situation or need to counsel a friend.

- **Service.** It certainly takes discipline to serve others—and Jesus tells us in Matthew 25 that when we serve others, we are serving him. Feel stagnant and disconnected from Jesus? Serve those he created.

- **Simplicity.** In a complicated, cluttered world, living with simplicity may sound radical, but it is a choice that lessens the physical noise in our lives. Practicing simplicity helps eat away at the hold materialism has on our lives.

- **Spiritual direction.** One of the greatest gifts I've given myself recently is investing in a spiritual director, who listens alongside me for what God is saying. When I can't seem to find God in a particular conundrum, she helps me be still enough to discern his direction and voice. Christians need each other—and there are those in the body of Christ who are trained to help us encounter Jesus.
- **Worship.** Praising God amid stressful storms or making it a practice to sing no matter what you face helps remind you that God is God and you are not.

Exploring spiritual disciplines doesn't have to be stressful. My hope is that highlighting a variety of them is invitational. Which ones resonate with you? What would bring you joy? These practices are simply a way to connect with God and grow in your relationship with the Storyteller of your life. To be restoried is to know him well—and with joy.

Be a Story Receiver

Once you've connected with Jesus in your discipleship story, your denouement turns outward, toward the people Jesus created. What does it look like to receive other people's stories with grace and intention? How can you reorient yourself toward others' needs?

In my early years of healing from a difficult past, I had a hard time receiving other people's stories. I was so broken that I out-trauma-ed them, upping the ante to gain attention for my terrible story. My empathy didn't have a chance to develop because I was so brokenhearted and needy.

Though it took decades, the more I healed, the more open I became to the stories of others. And the more I realized I had been restoried to become a restory-er. Because I had walked through hell and back (more than a few times), I could sit with a friend who had also experienced pain. The cool thing? The pain did not have to be the same.

Second Corinthians 1 demonstrates what happens when we become story receivers:

- *God gives us all the comfort we need.* He is full of mercy. "All praise to God, the Father of our Lord Jesus Christ. God is our merciful Father and the source of all comfort" (2 Corinthians 1:3).
- *He settles our hearts in* all *our conflicts.* The natural outpouring of his comfort is our transformation into comforters like him. There's a conduit of comfort, flowing from him to us, then through us. "He comforts us in all our troubles so that we can comfort others. When they are troubled, we will be able to give them the same comfort God has given us" (2 Corinthians 1:4).
- *An abundance of suffering is met with a superabundance of God's kindness toward us.* "The more we suffer for Christ, the more God will shower us with his comfort through Christ" (2 Corinthians 1:5).
- *There is heavenly reciprocity at play.* We receive, then joyfully give. Our comfort then informs other people's ability to endure trials. "Even when we are weighed down with troubles, it is for your comfort and salvation! For when we ourselves are comforted, we will certainly comfort you. Then you can patiently endure the same things we suffer" (2 Corinthians 1:6).
- *There is confidence in knowing that this outflow of God toward us in our pain will start a chain reaction in the body of Christ.*

> "We are confident that as you share in our sufferings, you will also share in the comfort God gives us" (2 Corinthians 1:7).

Moving from story giver (telling your story) to story receiver (being with others in their stories) is an important aspect of the sanctification journey—from inward healing to outward advocacy and compassion. If you're not at that place right now, please don't berate yourself. Healing takes an exceptionally long time, and sometimes we must retreat and rest before we can bear the weight of others' stories. When my husband and I walked away from our church of over two decades, I naïvely thought I could immediately step into the role of pastoring all the other people who had been harmed by that church. The effort bowled me over. I lost perspective. I forgot that first we must have a strong story of healing before we jump into the lives of hurting people. I had to give myself grace, reminding myself that *I* was a hurting person in need of someone else's ear.

That's the beauty of reciprocity. Sometimes we are broken and in need of restoration. And other times we have the wherewithal (through the Holy Spirit) to help another person who is hurting. Though Paul wrote the following words from 2 Corinthians 8 in relation to financially helping others in the body of Christ, the principles beneath demonstrate some universal truths about how we relate with one another:

- *We give only what we have.* If we are languishing and we have little to give, that's okay. In fact, it's normal, given the seasons we walk through in this life. We have seasons of abundance and seasons of lack. "You should finish what you started. Let the eagerness you showed in the beginning be matched now by your giving. Give in proportion to what you have" (2 Corinthians 8:11).

- *There is joy in giving—eagerly.* "Whatever you give is acceptable if you give it eagerly. And give according to what you have, not what you don't have" (2 Corinthians 8:12).
- *The Kingdom of God operates with a nondemanding reciprocity.* "Of course, I don't mean your giving should make life easy for others and hard for yourselves. I only mean that there should be some equality" (2 Corinthians 8:13).
- *We are not called to burn out when we give to others.* "Right now you have plenty and can help those who are in need. Later, they will have plenty and can share with you when you need it. In this way, things will be equal" (2 Corinthians 8:14).
- *There is an enoughness to God and the way he provides for us.* God is sufficient and can care for us, giving us the ability (through the Spirit) to care for others out of our abundance. "As the Scriptures say, / 'Those who gathered a lot had nothing left over, / and those who gathered only a little had enough'" (2 Corinthians 8:15).

Choose Small and Tend Large

Unfortunately, much of what is written about discipleship today has more to do with systems that create large numbers on a grand scale rather than the model of Jesus. I'm still astounded that the entire world was turned topsy-turvy not with a crowd but with a small group of followers. Jesus chose to pour himself into a few, who then replicated that model on a small scale. Discipleship is a connected, personal, social endeavor, where other people see the conduct and faithfulness of your life. It is caught, not necessarily taught in a classroom or memorized in a series of verses.

Once I was overwhelmed by my backyard garden. The thought of weeding the whole thing, particularly in the Texas heat, made me shudder. It was then I sensed God say, "Choose small and tend large." So I tackled a four-foot-by-eight-foot section of the vegetable garden and tended the heck out of it. In that smaller framework, I could thoroughly transform a small space. And you know what? I felt much better, even though the rest of the yard hollered at me to please weed it.

The world we live in is overwhelmingly large. We cannot possibly tend to its spiritual needs alone. But we can tend what God has put in front of us. You are the only you in your particular family. You are the only one in that specific position at your job. You're the only parent, friend, grandparent, aunt, uncle, or companion to that group of people. God has strategically placed you where you are for you to flourish there, no matter the smallness of the numbers.

Think of Rahab and her placement in history. She was simply faithful with what little she knew about God. She served the people in front of her (the spies, her family). This small obedience spurred a great deliverance and a royal lineage leading to the birth of Christ. We can never really judge our impact by numbers. As Jesus told us, "Those who are last now will be first then, and those who are first will be last" (Matthew 20:16). Those who seem to have a spectacular reach may not actually be bearing Kingdom fruit. And those who seem obscure may be quietly (secretly) pouring into the lives of people who will then do the same for others—in a great Kingdom chain reaction that is more grassroots movement than spectacle.

So how does Jesus' discipleship model (a few well-poured-into people) empower you to make lasting change in this world?

Friend, everything you do is chronicled by the One who sees you. Nothing is expended in vain. Your work, powered by the Spirit within, is creating beautifully unimaginable heavenly dividends. Your task? Simply be faithful to the story he's writing in you. My husband's life verse is instructive here: "My life is worth nothing to me unless

I use it for finishing the work assigned me by the Lord Jesus—the work of telling others the Good News about the wonderful grace of God" (Acts 20:24). Jesus has given you a you-shaped assignment, and your fulfillment of his great commission will be wildly different from anyone else's. Part of growing in Christ is recognizing that we are not called to cookie-cutter ministry and often our contributions don't end up looking the way we envisioned them beforehand.

When my family planted a church in France, I had expectations of what it would look like for me to be a minister overseas. The reality was starkly different. Mostly I cried. And struggled. And felt inadequate and illiterate. Looking back on it, I see that my ministry was simply one of presence—of loving my children and husband and the few friends the Lord brought my way. This was in no way splashy or full of praise. It was quite ordinary—but beautiful.

Join Safe Community

The deeper we grow in our relationships with Jesus, the more we are restoried, the better we become at discerning safe people and places. We cannot thrive in isolation, nor can we heal if we stay boundaryless in predatory relationships. Did you know that you are worth having strong, healthy relationships? You, as an image bearer of God, should be loved, cherished, and fought for. You deserve a haven. Of course, your primary haven is the Lord, who loves you, but he loves to encourage us with people who enhance our lives, bear our burdens, want what is best for us, and pray us toward health.

Demonstrate Your Faith

A difficult story does not disqualify you from growth; it's the catalyst for it. Weakness is not a liability but a doorway. We can always demonstrate our faith, even when we feel small, scared, tired, or brokenhearted. Often I feel like I must do grandiose acts of faith to be a qualified Christian, but the Lord is quite interested in small obedience over a lifetime. It's those little steps, walked in weakness, that demonstrate the habit of faith day in and day out. This is our personal denouement, the walking out of our faith.

In my book *You Can Raise Courageous and Confident Kids*, I write about the simplicity of walking out our faith (quite literally):

> [Jesus] walked to many villages with His disciples, practicing *peripatetic* spirituality. *Peripateo* is a common Greek word used widely in the New Testament with two primary meanings. One is to walk around, to circumvent, to walk, to go about. Jesus did a lot of this type of *peripateo* with His disciples. He walked on dusty paths. He ascended mountains with His followers. He ambled alongside them. He spent time. He was present. I find it fascinating that Jesus didn't start His formal ministry on earth until He had first been present, rubbing shoulders with mankind for 30 years.
>
> The other meaning of *peripateo* is the manner in which someone conducts his life, the way he lives and behaves. The apostle Paul used this word a lot: "As a prisoner for the Lord, then, I urge you to *live* a life worthy of the calling you have received" (Ephesians 4:1). "Join with others in following my example, brothers, and take note of those who *live* according to the pattern I gave you" (Philippians 3:17).[7]

In *The Writing Life*, Annie Dillard astutely reminds us that the way we live our lives daily makes up the quality of our lives: "How we spend our days is, of course, how we spend our lives. What we do with this hour, and that one, is what we are doing."[8] She goes on to write that tasks are the scaffolding of our days. I love the idea that our daily habits create a place for our days to land, even if our scaffolding feels like toothpicks. Because that's the gist of the restoried life—our weakness woven into God's strength. As Paul writes to the Corinthian believers,

> We now have this light shining in our hearts, but we ourselves are like fragile clay jars containing this great treasure. This makes it clear that our great power is from God, not from ourselves.
>
> We are pressed on every side by troubles, but we are not crushed. We are perplexed, but not driven to despair. We are hunted down, but never abandoned by God. We get knocked down, but we are not destroyed. Through suffering, our bodies continue to share in the death of Jesus so that the life of Jesus may also be seen in our bodies.
>
> 2 CORINTHIANS 4:7-10

Friend, you may feel like the fragility of your life disqualifies you from growth, but it's actually the catalyst for it. Those times you feel like death will win? Those are the avenues of grace, the stages of God's greatest faithfulness.

Demonstrating our faith in little increments through the habits of our lives is our practice of quiet evangelism. We are not called to be spectacular but faithful. Oswald Chambers writes, "I am called to live in perfect relation to God so that my life produces a longing after God in other lives, not admiration for myself. Thoughts about myself hinder my usefulness to God. God is not after perfecting me to be a specimen in His show-room; He is getting me to the place where He can use me."[9] The end is not our perfection; it's our connectedness to the One who is perfectly loving.

Restorying Rahab

Our denouements are works in progress. And we may not even grasp the amazing things God will do with our slow obedience and faithfulness as we walk out our faith. Like Rahab, we are still in the middle of our stories with life beckoning us forward. The ramifications of our obedience and suffering and healing are somewhat unknown. But every step we take matters—even if it's a baby step, even if we stumble backward, even when we doubt or grow discouraged. The point of our stories is how the Author is working all things out, tirelessly, kindly, beautifully.

Questions for Discussion

1. How does Rahab demonstrate a surprising and powerful denouement?
2. What are some ways you can incorporate quiet in your life?
3. Point out a recurring theme in your discipleship journey. What have you struggled with most? Whom have you most gravitated toward? What pitfalls have you encountered? What has come easily to you?
4. Which spiritual disciplines come naturally to you? Which ones intrigue you? Which one would you like to try this week? Why?

[illegible] been done [illegible] to let another story [illegible] others, and the wisdom of [illegible]

Self-editing your [illegible] monster, [illegible]

In short, you may try to [illegible] ders of [illegible] and surpass you, leaving you [illegible] place, unable to move beyo[illegible] it. Letting your story [illegible] past [illegible] and then move on.

The [illegible] three different story structures is [illegible] your story upon. It could be simple [illegible] (the inverted V) [illegible] pivot point in your life. Just tell [illegible] might want to "chunkify" [illegible] -year increments, highlighting the [illegible] relationships that shaped [illegible] decades. The climax can be anything you want—when you [illegible], when you got married, when you had children, or that reco[illegible] you accomplished last week. There will be a pivot point to your story, a clear before, and after. [illegible] fifteen [illegible] traumatic [illegible] early life [illegible] Jesus at fifteen, and I've been living in the [illegible] "Work to show the results of [illegible] with deep reverence and fear" (Philippians 2:12). [illegible] my restory began, and to be quite honest, [illegible] feeling you [illegible] In that case, or a circle on a piece of paper with the words I've shared in the [illegible] your [illegible] beginning. Detail wh[illegible] you met along the way, when you felt the call to something differe[illegible] what kind of difficulties and obstacles you faced. Did you have a mom[illegible] of profound change? And what does your life look like now that you've learned so much and you're helping others with their restorying?

The chiastic structure may take a little more thought. What wa[illegible] [illegible]

NINE

Discover the Power of Your Restoried Life

Success is not final. Failure is not fatal.
It's the courage to continue that counts.
ANONYMOUS

The Woman at the Well

Why did the man ask me for water?

Stunned by his strange request, I said, "You are a Jew, and I am a Samaritan woman. Why are you asking me for a drink?" The strange audacity of the man compelled me while the sun relentlessly pressed upon us both.

Next to the ancient well, he held my eyes. A smile crinkled there. "If you only knew the gift God has for you and who you are speaking to," he said, "you would ask me, and I would give you living water."

I told him this was an impossibility—after all, he had no container, no rope. I said, "And besides, do you think you're greater than our ancestor Jacob, who gave us this well? How can you offer better water than he and his sons and his animals enjoyed?" It was a fair question, a logical one. Sweat trickled down my cheek.

He spoke of our frailty—that we might drink water, but then the satiation ebbs, and we must begin the cycle of drawing water again. And again.

I wondered what he would say next because these words were true. I looked at my hands, roughened by the many trips I had made to that well just to keep myself alive.

"But those who drink the water I give will never be thirsty again. It becomes a fresh, bubbling spring within them, giving them eternal life." He looked beyond me toward the sky, as if to emphasize eternity. The sky, I knew, had no borders.

I asked him to please give me this magical water. I had grown so weary of carting water daily, and my life felt rote as my heart exhausted itself.

That's when the stranger turned the conversation away from eternal water to my daily world. "Go and get your husband," he said.

Panic rose inside me. Why would he ask such a thing? Why did he care? Was this a trick? Was there an appropriate answer I had to say to gain secret entrance to this abundant-water well? When I looked again in his eyes, squinting under the sun, I knew I could not lie to him. "I don't have a husband," I said.

He confirmed what I said, then added, "For you have had five husbands, and you aren't even married to the man you're living with now. You certainly spoke the truth!"

Now I knew he was a prophet, and I told him so. As a Samaritan, I know my place in the hierarchy in our region. But I thought, perhaps, I could ask a clarifying question: "Why is it that you Jews insist that Jerusalem is the only place of worship, while we Samaritans claim it is here at Mount Gerizim, where our ancestors worshiped?"

He called me a dear woman, something I will treasure all my life. I had been used and discarded by so many men, but here was a living water–giving man who called me dear. He pointed toward Jerusalem, then opened wide his arms as if to embrace the whole of our world. "The time is coming—indeed it's here now—when true worshipers will worship the Father in spirit and in truth." He continued, "The Father is looking for those who will worship him that way. For God is Spirit, so those who worship him must worship in spirit and in truth."

This confused me, and for a long pause I said nothing. But something in my heart told me that the man I stood before was no normal prophet. Could it be that he knew about the promised Messiah? I told him plainly, "I know the Messiah is coming—the one who is called Christ. When he comes, he will explain everything to us."

The sun continued its course in the sky. The sound of birdsong halted in that pregnant pause. The dust swirled at our feet as the wind picked up. A single cloud, puffy and insistent, graced the sky. I know because the moment demanded I pay attention.

"I AM the Messiah!" the man said.

I sucked in a breath, held it. Marveled. Stunned to silence. Could it be?

His companions returned, and with them, the familiar disdain in their eyes for a woman like me. Their friend had deigned to speak to me, a person clearly below his stature and importance—a Samaritan no less, quite unloved and ridiculed by the Jews.

But their judgment was of no consequence. I left my water bucket behind, ran to my town, and proclaimed to anyone who would listen, "Come and see a man who told me everything I ever did! Could he possibly be the Messiah?" I led a processional to the man, who is called Jesus, and my fellow Samaritans hung upon his words. We entreated him to stay with us, and he did for two days, teaching us about the Kingdom of God and healing our diseases. He cleansed several from unclean demonic spirits. One of my countrymen told me, "Now we believe, not just because of what you told us, but because we have heard him ourselves. Now we know that he is indeed the Savior of the world."

I had once been emptied, but now I'm filled.

I had once been marginalized by men, but now I'm empowered by One.

I had once felt the sting of alienation, but now I'm part of a holy nation.

I had once felt shame for my story, but now I can't help but tell the best story.

I had once been alone, but now I have community and purpose.

I have been utterly restoried.

You may feel like you're unworthy of a restory, but that is not true. Our great God loves to intersect the stories of all people—no matter where they find themselves. In fact, he seems to do his most beautiful work in those who seem to be the most unlikely candidates for renewal.

To receive a new story is to emulate the woman at the well, to come to Jesus with nothing but leave filled.

I have this urge to want to complete things in my life: not merely my actions but actual things. If I notice I am missing part of a set, I must complete it. If my wardrobe is missing a black blazer, I spend an inordinate amount of time finding a replacement so my closet can be whole. The woman at the well, similarly, was theoretically trying to refill her life every day through the most rudimentary of journeys. She was thirsty—she needed a drink. But day by day she thirsted again, so she made the trek. Day in and day out, every week, every month, every year. But then she met the kind stranger who asked her to set aside her own needs for a moment and give him a drink.

Similarly, when Jesus approaches us, he asks us to shift from self-focus to looking to the needs of others. To follow him is costly—it involves sacrifice and relinquishing what we think we need. But in return? We are filled with living water. The thirst within us is satiated. We are complete. Whole.

There's a striking prophecy by the prophet Jeremiah that describes our state before we are restoried. "My people have done two evil things: / They have abandoned me— / the fountain of living water. / And they have dug for themselves cracked cisterns / that can hold no water at all!" (Jeremiah 2:13). When we live our lives apart from the Lord, we forsake the source of living water. But we are still a thirsty people. We continue to have the pesky need to drink. So instead of relishing a relationship with God, who supplies us with living water, we resort to our own ingenuity and scrappiness. We dig a big ol' hole, line it with concrete, then pray for rain.

The problem is, when we create a cistern of our own, we forget the pesky nature of the shifting earth. Factors outside our control allow the earth to imperceptibly rumble and then crack the cistern. Though we can spend too much time repairing all the holes created by the fallenness of this world, we have a problem. Even if the rain comes, it slips through each emerging hole, leaving us without water and parched. That's where we meet the woman at the well—and that place of need is where Jesus met her.

That is where he meets you, too.

At your point of need.

Thirsty.

Weary from digging holes that sprout leaks.

The restory journey begins with a conversation with Jesus, who is the only One who can fill you up, complete you, and heal you. He will expose those areas of weariness, frustration, and sin—but *not* in a way that brings shame. No, he offers the hope of a new life, a new way of navigating this difficult world. His is the kind of strength, administered through the Holy Spirit, that can sustain you through trials and stressors and difficulties and enemies and pain. His is not a superficial balm but the deepest kind of cleansing and healing from the inside out. Note that Jesus didn't ask the Samaritan woman to change—he invited her to a brand-new life, where change would come because he had changed her. And that brand-new life ignited her toward the care and keeping of others.

Her response to this cataclysmic shift was to turn outward toward rescue.

She wanted others to be filled.

She couldn't help but pursue the hearts of her townspeople.

She had been so believed, received, and redeemed that she wanted that for others.

Funny things happen when Jesus satiates you. All that energy you used to spend trying to complete your story through idols, broken cisterns, vain pursuits, and people you hoped would fill you is now freed up! You can move on from your position of abandonment to a place of abundance.

Our capacity for helping others enlarges the more we experience Jesus and his filling. Not only that, but God is expanding our capacity for the beauty of heaven. That's what our restory journeys are for—to grow our hearts bigger for people here on earth and to prepare us for the wild and full redemption awaiting us on the other side.

Liminal Space

When the Lord whispered the word *restory* into my mind, I had no idea where it would take me. Since that time, I've hosted two Restory Conferences (where I had the privilege of watching Jesus change lives), pioneered a podcast (where I featured everyday folks who have experienced their own restorying), written many books, and spent a decade walking out my own restory journey. I've fallen in love with the Scriptures again through rapid reading, and I've grown to adore theology, particularly the big story of God in the Bible. And I've seen God take the ashes of my life (oh, so many ashes!) and use them as fertilizer for his next work through me. One little word toward me, backed by the ardent heart of God, has changed everything about my life. That's my prayer for you, too.

Here on earth, we haven't reached the conclusion of our stories—yet. We live between the *now* and the *not yet.* And in that liminal place, we walk the restory journey, restoried from the past, redeemed for the present, and prepared for the future.

Restoried from the Past

To move from living our lives in retrospect toward proactively following God's beckoning future, we must look backward and discern what we need to learn.

One day my friend D'Ann helped me with this exercise when she slid a spiral-bound packet of note cards across the table to me. She vulnerably shared how she'd spent her life believing lies about herself—so much so that the lies had overpowered any truth the Lord wanted to speak into her life. These were beliefs she felt were untrue but couldn't shake. And they didn't square with the Word of God.

"I want you to take these." She fanned the cards between us now. "On one side write the lie you're believing; then on the back ask the Lord to combat that lie by giving you Scriptures that counteract it. It may not be easy at first. It took me a long time. But once I'd done it, I spent time reading through those cards, reminding myself of the truth."

Honestly, at the time I didn't feel like I had a problem with lies. But she reminded me that hidden lies tend to be insidious and that they arise from our upbringings. They can feel true because the people in our lives have either said them or have lived as if they were true. This made more sense to me. For the sake of brevity, I'll share three of mine:

- *Lie 1:* I am abandoned, and no one will help me.
- *Lie 2:* I deserve rejection, neglect, and abuse.
- *Lie 3:* I am worth absolutely nothing.

These lies came directly from my own story. When I whispered to the babysitter that I was being abused and she said she told my mom, I believed her. But when my mom failed to intervene, this belief of abandonment cemented into my soul. I also felt like rejection, neglect, and abuse happened to me because there was something fundamentally flawed in my person. Other children deserved happy lives, kindhearted and intentional parents, and nurture, but I must've done something wrong since I didn't have these things. I could only daydream of a happy family life—one that never, ever came. Perhaps this explains my penchant for watching *Little House on the Prairie* reruns and playacting that series with my best friend. We both longed for "normal" families with connected parents. Since we didn't have them in our real lives, we pretended.

All that pain, neglect, and abuse led me to a strong, horrible conclusion: I had no worth—except, maybe, if I tried to earn it through excelling. My only worth came from performance, but even that became a tenuous endeavor. The moment I failed, I lost all worth.

I have heard that navigating stress well means choosing which thoughts I dwell on. In my quest to uncover lies and retrain my mind with the truth, I had to learn to actively choose a different way of thinking. Without realizing it, I was self-practicing cognitive behavioral therapy, which the Mayo Clinic describes as helping you "become aware of thinking patterns that may be creating issues in your life."[1]

The Bible also affirms this way of working through the past:

> Don't copy the behavior and customs of this world, but let God transform you into a new person by changing the way you think. Then you will learn to know God's will for you, which is good and pleasing and perfect.
> ROMANS 12:2

> We destroy every proud obstacle that keeps people from knowing God. We capture their rebellious thoughts and teach them to obey Christ.
> 2 CORINTHIANS 10:5

It is difficult but important work to sift through your past, asking God to uncover the lies you've believed. Here's how I reframed my three lies with truth statements and Scripture verses:

> *Lie 1:* I am abandoned, and no one will help me.
> *Truth 1:* Even if others abandon me, Jesus will not.
>
> Even if my father and mother abandon me,
> the Lord will hold me close.
> PSALM 27:10

> *Lie 2:* I deserve rejection, neglect, and abuse.
> *Truth 2:* God gives me dignity.
>
> I praise you because I am fearfully and wonderfully made;
> your works are wonderful,
> I know that full well.
> PSALM 139:14, NIV

Lie 3: I am worth absolutely nothing.
Truth 3: I am worthy because of Jesus.

"You must let little children come to me, and you must never stop them. The kingdom of Heaven belongs to little children like these!"
MATTHEW 19:14, PHILLIPS

A friend of mine once wrote in an email, "I'm the creation of a loving God. By repeating . . . negative words, I insult wonderful work." I had to understand just how soul destroying those lies were to me—and that when I believed them as the truth, I pushed against the healing God wanted to bring to my life.

The problem is that we are like caterpillars inching through very tall grass, each blade imprinted with lies. We cannot perceive they are lies because we live among them; they are our environment. Only when we are radically changed from chrysalis to butterfly can we soar above them and begin to see them for what they really are. The higher we soar, the tinier the lies become. In that aerial place, we can finally start our new lives based on heavenly truth.

With truth as your new atmosphere, you can better discern lies for what they are. They're no longer big or scary or permeating your life; they're blessedly manageable. We see this butterfly-like transformation in Ephesians 2:4-7:

God is so rich in mercy, and he loved us so much, that even though we were dead because of our sins, he gave us life when he raised Christ from the dead. (It is only by God's grace that you have been saved!) For he raised us from the dead along with Christ and seated us with him in the heavenly realms because we are united with Christ Jesus. So God can point to

> us in all future ages as examples of the incredible wealth of his grace and kindness toward us, as shown in all he has done for us who are united with Christ Jesus.

We are no longer crawling on our bellies in the quagmire of the past—we are soaring in the heavenly realms. The old has gone, and the new life God has for us awaits (2 Corinthians 5:17). The hinge point between the two is blessed resurrection.

We were lost. Now we are found.

We were dead. Now we are alive.

We were disgraced. Now we are graced.

We were alone. Now we are welcomed into God's family.

We were orphans. Now we are adopted by our good God.

We were hopeless. Now we are filled with eschatological hope.

Author Joshua Hook once shared with me about a picture he'd found of himself as a child on a carnival train ride. He looked happy, engaged. Joshua said,

> We have painful experiences, and then we tell a painful story about ourselves. I'm stupid. I can't do anything right. I'm worthless. I'm too . . . fat, skinny, short, tall, loud, quiet, etc. And the story becomes our reality and dictates the rest of our lives. What I love about the little guy driving the train is that it was me before I had a chance to develop any of those painful stories about myself. I was curious, loud, playful, open, connected, and smart. I want to get in touch with that little guy, rediscover my true self, and shed the painful stories I have continued to tell about myself over the years.[2]

This is our task, friend. To become childlike in the best possible way—to become open, alive, joyful, and anticipatory. But to do that we have to uncover the lies of the past and do the hard work of disentangling them.

Redeemed for the Present

We live in the great *right now*—in this moment, as you're reading this. God wants to restory us today, to give us a redeemed perspective currently. He is the Great I AM, not I WAS—he is ever present, able to empower, encourage, and enthrall us. As we consider our next steps in this adventure, I've created some questions to help you frame where you are today:

- In a culture deeply invested in narrative, how can you tell a compelling Jesus story that winsomely invites growth, healing, change, and peace?
- How does your story intersect with God's Kingdom story?
- What does it mean to be a proactive character in your own growth story?
- How can you encourage others to chase after Jesus in an intentional way?
- What elements of your past story can you see God using right now?
- What elements of your present story would you like to see God heal?
- Where are you in the story of the woman at the well? Empty? Conversing with your Savior? Redeemed? Telling others about his amazingness?
- If someone else were retelling your story to others, how would they frame it? What would they emphasize?

- What do you wish your story communicated?
- Where are you in your relationship with Jesus? Do you feel close to him? Alienated? Angry? Indifferent? Stressed? Settled? Disappointed? Confused?

Take some time to ponder the answers to these questions, because they will help you understand where you are. You cannot move on if you don't first define where you are in the story of your life. Today is pregnant with potential. Though our stories are formed in our pasts, we live and work out those stories in the present. God redeems us for the beautiful now.

Prepared for the Future

We may live today in the moment, but every aspect of our lives is part of the preparation God is doing in and through us for what we will face in the future. Today is tomorrow's training ground. When we are faithful today, that spills over into tomorrow's faithfulness. If you're anxious about tomorrow (who isn't?), remember that God is weaving through you a new kind of resilience to face pain and issues as they arise.

In light of that truth, it's a good exercise to ask ourselves questions about who we want to be, or who we envision ourselves becoming in the future, through the transformative power of the Holy Spirit. Consider these things:

- Which qualities of the fruit of the Spirit (love, joy, peace, patience, kindness, goodness, faithfulness, gentleness, self-control; Galatians 5:22-23) are hardest for you? What would you like to see the Lord do in your life in one of these areas? What would it look like, for example, for future you to live as a kindhearted person? A joyful follower of Jesus? One who exercises self-control?

- What kind of ministry that you haven't had a chance to try appeals to you?
- What would it look like for you to be financially fit in the future?
- How would you like your social life to grow? Shrink?
- Where do you see your vocation being played out in ten years?
- What would a peaceful, restful way of life look like to you?
- How would letting go of bitterness and embracing the journey of forgiveness positively affect your relationships?
- What familial relationships do you want to be pouring into?
- What boundaries do you need to enact to protect yourself from being repeatedly injured by someone?
- What little habits can you implement now that, compounded over time, would make a big difference?
- What lifestyle changes would you like to incorporate in your daily walk with God?
- Would getting counseling, spiritual direction, prayer, or the opportunity to go on a retreat help you get beyond that stuck place you're experiencing?
- What makes a life meaningful, in your opinion?
- What drains you currently?
- What triggers do you still react to? How can working through those help future you?

I believe in God's great ability to restory you, friend. In one of my life's Scripture passages, Psalm 40:1-3, David recounts the *past*, the *now*, and the *not yet*. His words are my hope for you on your own restory adventure, and they fit perfectly the journey we've been on throughout this book:

- To experience a new story, we have to *want* to experience change. We must ask God for help. This takes patience and tenacity. "I waited patiently for the Lord to help me, / and he turned to me and heard my cry" (verse 1).
- When we come to the end of ourselves, that's when God does the heavy lifting of rescuing us and setting us on our way. "He lifted me out of the pit of despair, / out of the mud and the mire. / He set my feet on solid ground / and steadied me as I walked along" (verse 2).
- Once we've been transformed, God gives us a *So what?* to our stories to lead others toward him. "He has given me a new song to sing, / a hymn of praise to our God. / Many will see what he has done and be amazed. / They will put their trust in the Lord" (verse 3).

The Good News

You are not disqualified because of a difficult story or stories. You are not sidelined because of your pain. You are growing into someone who is learning to trust yourself, empowered to use your voice, and eager to make an impact on the community around you.

Perhaps you're struggling as you read this last chapter. Maybe you're tired or your soul feels injured. You have been on this healing journey a long time, and you feel stuck or world-weary. What you are feeling is normal, and these emotions will not last forever. Feeling stuck is not the same as remaining stuck. But even if you feel unmotivated to take the tiniest step toward a restory, remember that you can always honestly pray, *Lord, please help me want to change. Or maybe better said—help me want to want to change.* God loves answering us in our fatigue and discouragement.

Or maybe you have absorbed the belief that healing is selfish, introspective, or narcissistic. Friend, it is not. Your healing journey is the very best gift you give to your friends and family, who desperately need a healed you. If you can't walk the restory journey for yourself, do it for them. Restorying is a benevolent endeavor. It changes not only the trajectory of your life but also that of the next generations. It's your hard work of creating a legacy—something utterly different than what you've inherited. Your upbringing and hard times do not disqualify you from this life; they are the gateway you must pass through (as everyone must) to experience the help, power, and healing of Jesus.

To become who we are—fully alive and free—we must come to the end of who we were. I mentioned one of my life Scripture passages earlier in this chapter, and I'll end with another. The apostle Paul speaks of weakness and perceived worthlessness in the hands of a redeeming, restorying God:

> Remember, dear brothers and sisters, that few of you were wise in the world's eyes or powerful or wealthy when God called you. Instead, God chose things the world considers foolish in order to shame those who think they are wise. And he chose things that are powerless to shame those who are powerful. God chose things despised by the world, things counted as nothing at all, and used them to bring to nothing what the world considers important. As a result, no one can ever boast in the presence of God.
>
> 1 CORINTHIANS 1:26-29

Do you see it? God isn't looking for the cool kids. He's not seeking the most intelligent or accomplished. He doesn't do his best redemptive work through the strong and powerful. No, he is seeking *you*, the weakened one, the despised, the rejected. Why? Because you will give him the glory for the new story he creates. We wrongly believe that our weakness points to our frailty and disqualification. But it's a doorway instead. Here is the truth: "The eyes of the LORD search the whole earth in order to strengthen those whose hearts are fully committed to him" (2 Chronicles 16:9). God is looking for people who know their need for him.

That's the qualifying narrative.

We are weak. He is strong.

People have tried to destroy us, but he is in the process of restorying us.

We may be broken by our stories, but God knows how to reframe them—not merely for our sake but also for the sake of this world he loves.

Restorying the Woman at the Well

This is the Good News. God takes the ramshackled, messy ones, sets their feet upon his steady rock, cleans them up, then sends them out to help others. This is what Jesus did with the woman at the well. He spoke to her, told her the truth, then utterly changed her life through their long interaction. She became a zealous missionary to her village, proclaiming the ability of Jesus to know a life. She was restoried in order to tell a better story to the outcast Samaritans—that they would be welcomed into this new Kingdom Jesus preached.

Like the woman at the well, you have a truly unique story. Only you have those particular inciting incidents. Only you have experienced those specific trials and traumas along the way. Only you have had that exact encounter with Christ. Only you know all the people in your circle of community. Only you fill your life with these specific activities. And so you have a special you-shaped calling upon your life. Step into it. Dare to heal from the past. Embrace the possibilities of today. Like the woman at the well, go into your city and tell people about how God has restoried you.

The best revenge after pain is a joyful life.

> If anyone is in Christ, he is a new creation; what is old has passed away—look, what is new has come!
>
> 2 CORINTHIANS 5:17, NET

Questions for Discussion

1. What are some of the lies you've believed, particularly about your worth and your place in the world?
2. What truths have you uncovered about who you are in Jesus Christ by reading Scripture? How have those truths set you free?
3. How does the woman at the well emulate the restory message?
4. What part of the restory message has most resonated with you? Why?
5. What new thing is Jesus doing in your life right now? What can you praise him for? What role does gratitude play in the restory adventure?

[illegible] push the

down [illegible]

[illegible] valley, it will then come

[illegible]

[illegible]

[illegible] may be [illegible]

to let out the story and make meaning [illegible]

others, and the wisdom of [illegible]

Self-editing your [illegible]

monster [illegible] or confronting [illegible]

In short, you may try to [illegible] the [illegible] with [illegible] you and [illegible] you leaving you [illegible] place, unable to grow beyond it. Letting out your story [illegible] out from under [illegible] your past and gives you a chance to [illegible] heal—and to move on.

The reason I [illegible] these three different story structures is to give you [illegible] in shaping your story. It can be a simple story [illegible] the inverted V [illegible] a large piece of [illegible] point in your life. [illegible] on your [illegible] you may want to [illegible] your story [illegible] highlighting the [illegible] relationships that shaped [illegible] when you [illegible] you [illegible] children, or that [illegible] pivot point to your story [illegible] a clear before and after. [illegible] fifteen [illegible] traumatic [illegible] life [illegible] Jesus [illegible] fifteen, and I've been living [illegible] working hard to show the results of my [illegible] with deep reverence and fear" (Philippians [illegible]) [illegible] restory again, and to be quite honest, I'm still [illegible] your [illegible] you relate more [illegible]. In that case, [illegible] a circle on a [illegible] piece of paper [illegible] words [illegible] in the [illegible] your birth [illegible] the story world's beginning. Detail who you met along the way, when you [illegible] to something different, what kind of difficulties and obstacles you faced. Did you have a mom[illegible] of profound change? And what does your life look like now that you've learned so much and you're helping others with their restorying?

The chiastic structure may take a little more thought. What was

CONCLUSION

The End, or the Beginning?

Move toward the next thing, not away from the last thing.
Same direction. Completely different energy.
JAMES CLEAR

My Friend Ashley

Yesterday, I went to therapy. I know I have this beautiful, abundant life that God intimately grafted me into. Yet, the pain from my past often robs me of the depth of joy available to me today.

My fear of vulnerability and helplessness evaporated when I thought about the alternative of not getting better. The reality that my unhealed wounds and trauma could ruin my current and future relationships sounded its siren loud enough for me to honestly get over myself and get help.

The other day, I had a conversation with an almost estranged family member who said, "I love you so much I would die for you." To which I countered, "But do you love me enough to heal for me?"

Then, I had to sit with that question, hold it up like a mirror, and see if I could say the same for those who love me the most.

And my answer is yes. Yes, I do love my people enough to heal for them. . . .

[Jesus] wants us to heal and He provides many means and pathways to help us find what we need. My journey may differ greatly from yours, and that's okay. But if you need permission or some sort of sign, I pray God would reveal to you as He did to me how He guided me to this very point in time.

I pray we see how much He is for us and wants us to experience the depths of His joy and abundance. Even if it means letting the light penetrate the darkest caverns of our minds and hearts.[1]

As a child, Robert Louis Stevenson saw lights from afar igniting as if out of nowhere. What he didn't know was that lamplighters were lighting the streetlights. Once it was properly explained it to him, he said that they were "punching holes in the darkness."[2] That's our task as we dare to heal. When I was a long way into my own journey, a friend emailed me, saying that God had changed me from a victim to a "carrier of light," and I think she's right. That's true of you, too.

But before we move toward illuminating others, something must end. Our old way of living, the prisons we live in, the darkness we've grown accustomed to—these must be crucified with Christ, then healed. We must learn to welcome Christ's white-hot light into the dark corners of our souls. The prophet Isaiah calls us forth: "I will say to the prisoners, 'Come out in freedom,' / and to those in darkness, 'Come into the light'" (Isaiah 49:9). This beckoning underlines the outward nature of the restoried life. Real freedom comes when we set others free.

In his book *The Rest of God*, author Mark Buchanan speaks of a difficult counseling session during which he heard a horrific story from a congregant. For a long while, he did not know what to say. He writes, "And then God slipped me an insight, timely as manna dropped from the sky. He showed me that her past was beyond repair, at least on my watch. If there was any good thing there to salvage, I knew not how. But in the same instant God showed me she still had her future. And it was vast, unbroken, pristine, radiant. . . . Her past was a tragedy to lament. But her future was an epic to anticipate."[3] That's the crux of the restory journey—that before us lies an anticipatory joy of what God will do next.

When I started speaking around the country and the world about this restory message, the visual God gave me was of a story printed on a piece of copier paper. It felt solid, real, true. But then the picture transformed into a person folding that story into a paper airplane and launching it into the unknown. I prayed through a list of words that define who we are as Jesus followers, then printed them out, one per sheet of paper. At the end of my restory message, each person would receive one of those words and then craft a paper airplane. I instructed each of them to keep it somewhere visible so they could remember what the Lord had said about them and rest in knowing that their story was not over—it was in the process of flying.

I want to end this book with those words. May these wash over you as you fold your story into flight—as God does what only he can do, creating a most unusual restory testimony in you.

Friend, you are

- a child of God
- abundant
- accepted
- adopted
- affirmed
- alive
- befriended
- beloved
- brightened
- changed
- cherished
- chosen
- clean
- defended
- delivered
- emancipated
- embraced
- empowered
- enduring
- enlivened
- filled
- forgiven
- freed
- fruitful

- healed
- heard
- held
- home
- joy filled
- light filled
- loved
- noticed
- nourished
- opened
- protected
- rebuilt
- redeemed
- remembered
- renewed
- rescued
- restored
- rewarded
- seen
- sought
- sustained
- understood
- wanted
- watered
- welcomed
- whole
- worthy

Now may the God of peace himself make you completely holy and may your spirit and soul and body be kept entirely blameless at the coming of our Lord Jesus Christ.

1 THESSALONIANS 5:23, NET

Acknowledgments

Thank you, Caitlyn Carlson, for asking me what I really felt passion for. This book contains what I love to teach—thanks to your questions and cheerleading. I am grateful for you, dear agent, Joy Eggerichs, for your continued tenacity and kindness as you pitched and repitched iterations of this book. I'm grateful for the whole team at NavPress and Tyndale for all they've done to champion this book. I'm humbled, really.

My prayer team, the Writing Prayer Circle, prays me through every book I've written. Profound thanks to Katharine, Claire, Zach, Matt, Stacey, Rod, Jenny, Chris, Amy V., Tabea, Robin, Sabrina, Misty, Audrey, Rebecca C., Patti, Cheryl E., Amy G., Elaine, Paula, Kendra, Yanci, Paul, Richard, Sue, Christy, Alice, Susie, TJ, Dorian, Colette, Patricia, Cheri, Gina, Jessica, Michelle N., Ellen, Lacy, Rebecca J., Lisa, Heidi, Becky S., Michelle W., Julie, Kristin, Becky O., Sabina, Anna, Leslie, Tosca, Sophie, Diane, Tim, Susan W., Cheryl R., Patrick, Holly, Cyndi, Katy, Judy, Erin, Jeanne, Caroline, Anita, Ralph, Hope, and Kelley. Your prayers have carried me through my own valley of bewilderment. Thank you.

Of course, no story is complete without characters. Thanks to Life Sentence, aka Leslie Wilson and D'Ann Mateer, who are truly in this writing gig for life. To my three adult kids: Sophie, Aidan, and Julia, who are the reason I wanted to reframe my story in the first place—thank you. And to Patrick, who has been my leading man all these years. My healing is interwoven with you. Thank you for loving me through so many pain points.

Jesus, you have truly rewritten my story. It's a privilege to live it every day and point to you.

Notes

ONE | MAP YOUR OWN STORY

1. Benjamin Hardy, *Willpower Doesn't Work: Discover the Hidden Keys to Success* (Hachette Books, 2019), 214.
2. Phil Cousineau, introduction to *The Hero's Journey: Joseph Campbell on His Life and Work*, by Joseph Campbell, ed. Phil Cousineau and Stuart L. Brown (Harper & Row, 1990), xvi.
3. Connie Angel Sanders, email message to author, June 11, 2024. Used by permission.
4. Robert B. Chisholm Jr., *Interpreting the Minor Prophets* (Academie Books, 1990), 12–13.

TWO | UNEARTH YOUR SETTING

1. Bessel van der Kolk, *The Body Keeps the Score: Brain, Mind, and Body in the Healing of Trauma* (Penguin Books, 2015).
2. *Merriam-Webster Dictionary*, "setting," accessed June 12, 2025, https://www.merriam-webster.com/dictionary/setting.
3. Benjamin Hardy, *Willpower Doesn't Work: Discover the Hidden Keys to Success* (Hachette Books, 2019), 136.
4. Van der Kolk, *The Body Keeps the Score.*
5. This list is based on an Instagram post I wrote. Mary DeMuth (@marydemuth), "9 Traits of a Safe Church," Instagram, August 28, 2024, https://www.instagram.com/marydemuth/p/C_NA-t6xzPj/?img_index=1.
6. "6 Trauma Responses: Fight, Flight, Freeze, Fawn, Fine, and Faint," The Attachment Project, accessed July 7, 2025, https://www.attachmentproject.com/psychology/trauma-response-types.
7. I explore this idea in *The Seven Deadly Friendships* but have given it more flesh here. Mary DeMuth, *The Seven Deadly Friendships: How to Heal When Painful Relationships Eat Away at Your Joy* (Harvest House, 2018), 153–62.

THREE | DISCOVER THE CHARACTERS IN YOUR STORY

1. "The Stoic Concept of Apatheia," The Stoic Store, March 3, 2023, https://www.stoicstore.co.uk/blogs/stoicism/the-stoic-concept-of-apatheia.
2. Quoted in "The Stoic Concept of Apatheia."
3. Shannon Waterman, email message to author, spring 2018. Used by permission.

FOUR | IDENTIFY YOUR INCITING INCIDENTS

1. From the Hebrew word *heḇel* (translated "meaningless" in the NLT).
2. "Things We Leave Behind," track 3 on Michael Card, *Poiēma*, Sparrow Records, 1994.
3. C. S. Lewis, *The Last Battle*, The Chronicles of Narnia (HarperTrophy, 2000), 195–97.
4. Henry Cloud, *Necessary Endings: The Employees, Businesses, and Relationships That All of Us Have to Give Up in Order to Move Forward* (Harper Business, 2010), 45–46.
5. Mark Buchanan, *Spiritual Rhythm: Being with Jesus Every Season of Your Soul* (Zondervan, 2010), 17.

FIVE | ENDURE THE MUDDLED MIDDLE

1. Holly Seddon, "The Unreliable Narrator: All You Need to Know," Jericho Writers, accessed June 19, 2025, https://jerichowriters.com/the-unreliable-narrator.

SEVEN | DISCOVER THE *SO WHAT?* OF YOUR STORY

1. Aaron Earls, "Unearthed Ancient Church Confirms Christianity's Rapid Spread to Africa," Lifeway Research, December 16, 2019, https://research.lifeway.com/2019/12/16/unearthed-ancient-church-confirms-Christianitys-rapid-spread-to-africa.
2. John Newton, "Amazing Grace," 1779.

EIGHT | WALK OUT YOUR STORY

1. Christopher Helton, "Your Words Matter: Sanctification," Sermons by Logos, August–October 2023, https://sermons.logos.com/sermons/1168041.
2. Jason Ruis, "Learning to Abide in God from 1 John," The Abide Project, November 15, 2021, https://www.abideproject.org/p/learning-to-abide-in-God-from-1-john.
3. Quoted in Marcel Schwantes, "Warren Buffett Says the People You Hang Out with Can Be the Difference Between Success and Failure. Here Are 3 Types You Need in Your Life," *Inc.*, April 26, 2023, https://www.inc.com/marcel-schwantes/warren-buffett-says-who-you-hang-out-with-can-be-difference-between-success-failure-here-are-3-types-of-people-you-need-in-your-life.html.

4. Brother Lawrence, *The Practice of the Presence of God* (Whitaker House, 1982), 37.
5. Madame Jeanne Guyon, *Experiencing God Through Prayer* (Whitaker House, 1984), 13.
6. I wrote a book about this experience: Mary DeMuth, *90-Day Bible Reading Challenge: Read the Whole Bible, Change Your Whole Life* (Bethany House, 2023).
7. Mary E. DeMuth, *You Can Raise Courageous and Confident Kids* (Harvest House, 2011), 60.
8. Annie Dillard, *The Writing Life* (Harper Perennial, 2013), 32. Emphasis added to quoted Scripture in source.
9. Oswald Chambers, *My Utmost for His Highest* (Barbour, 1935), 251.

NINE | DISCOVER THE POWER OF YOUR RESTORIED LIFE

1. "Cognitive Behavioral Therapy," Mayo Clinic, accessed February 26, 2025, https://www.mayoclinic.org/tests-procedures/cognitive-behavioral-therapy/about/pac-20384610.
2. Joshua Hook, email message to author, n.d. Used by permission.

CONCLUSION | THE END, OR THE BEGINNING?

1. Ashley Moore (@heyashleymoore), "Yesterday, I went to therapy," Instagram, June 13, 2024, https://www.instagram.com/heyashleymoore/reel/C8KQ13_xfCT.
2. Quoted in Skip Heitzig, "Punching Holes in the Darkness," Billy Graham Evangelistic Association of Canada, February 19, 2015, https://www.billygraham.ca/stories/punching-holes-in-the-darkness.
3. Mark Buchanan, *The Rest of God: Restoring Your Soul by Restoring Sabbath* (Thomas Nelson, 2006), 209–10.